Information Literacy

Information literacy is not just about finding information: it is a true catalyst for educational change. It enables independent lifelong learning. This conference considers how information professionals and academics can seek to engage students bewitched by quick and easy internet searching and move towards the information literate university.

Themes include:

- working towards the information literate university

- engaging the internet generation

- new ideas in information literacy teaching and learning

- developing partnerships in information literacy

- using information literacy as a positive driver for educational change

STAFFORDSHIRE
UNIVERSITY

Information Services

Information Literacy:

Recognising the Need

Staffordshire University
Stoke-on-Trent
United Kingdom
17 May 2006

Edited by
Geoff Walton and Alison Pope

Chandos Publishing
Oxford • England

Chandos Publishing (Oxford) Limited
Chandos House
5 & 6 Steadys Lane
Stanton Harcourt
Oxford OX29 5RL
UK
Tel: +44 (0) 1865 884447 Fax: +44 (0) 1865 884448
Email: info@chandospublishing.com
www.chandospublishing.com

First published in Great Britain 2006
ISBN: 1-84334-243-X (978-1-84334-243-4)
© The Authors, 2006

Produced from electronic copy supplied by authors.

Printed in the UK and USA.

Printed in the UK by 4edge Limited - www.4edge.co.uk

Contents

Background to the conference

Staffordshire University is well known for its commitment to supporting widening participation in higher education and the University's Information Services is pleased to be organising this one day event. It was prompted by the conferment of Learning and Teaching Fellowships on two of the University's Information Services staff, Alison Pope and Geoff Walton and also by the Information Services Learning Support Team's many years of activity across the skills agenda. This activity has especially focused upon the support and delivery of information literacy.

The event is independent of any outside organisation or group.

Information literacy: recognising the need

A national conference on the topic of information literacy
17th May 2006

Focusing on how to engage the internet generation this conference is aimed at librarians, information professionals and academic colleagues. Information literacy isn't just about finding information; it is a true catalyst for educational change. It enables independent lifelong learning. This conference considers how we can engage students and move towards the information literate University. The conference features seven nationally renowned speakers

Susie Andretta - Senior Lecturer in Information Management
London Metropolitan University.

Moira Bent - Faculty Liaison Librarian
University of Newcastle and National Learning and Teaching Fellow

Debbi Boden - Faculty Team Leader at Imperial College London

Sheila Corrall - Professor of Librarianship & Information Management at the University of Sheffield.

Peter Godwin - Academic Services Manager in Learning & Information Services at London South Bank University

Mark Hepworth - Lecturer in the Department of Information Science at Loughborough University

Sheila Webber - Senior Lecturer in the Department of Information Studies at the University of Sheffield

Their themes include

Using information literacy as a positive driver for educational change.
Developing partnerships in information literacy.
Training the trainers.
Engaging the Google generation.
New ideas in information literacy teaching and learning.
The information literate university.

These proceedings also include two additional papers from colleagues who did not speak at the conference. They are from Rosie Jones, Karen Peters and Emily Shields at Manchester Metropolitan University and Tony Brauer from Buckinghamshire Chilterns University College.

We would like to thank the following people for their help and support in organising this event; Julie Adams, Ron Allcock, Francine Bossons, Jan Bould, Jeanette Chadwick, Liz Hart, Dave Parkes, Derek Sheward, Marj Spiller, Janet Weaver and Helen Wells. We would like to extend our thanks to Staffordshire University Marketing Team and the many other people not listed here who also lent a hand, especially Katherine, Hannah and James.

Geoff Walton and Alison Pope
Learning and Teaching Fellows
Information Services
Staffordshire University

Information literacy: recognising the need - an introduction

Alison Pope - Information Services, Staffordshire University
Geoff Walton - Information Services, Staffordshire University

Context

The Government White Paper, January 2003, states that:
"As well as improving vocational skills, we need to ensure that all graduates, including those who study traditional academic disciplines, have the right skills to equip them for a lifetime in a fast changing work environment.'[1]

It is our view that, in addition to offering excellent academic courses, higher education institutions should aim to give students the chance to gain grounding in the skills which will support them in the future, both as citizens and employees. Many notably Bruce (1995) and Bundy (2004) argue that of all these skills, the need to be information literate is essential.

What is Information Literacy?

Information professionals throughout the world are familiar with the term *information literacy* and it has seen wide and varied use since the term was first coined by Paul Zirkowski in 1974 (Andretta, 2005). It has been observed by Owusu-Ansah (2003) that the information profession has, and continues to, put forward the information literacy, cause with a near-missionary zeal although there does exist a minority view which questions the worth of information literacy regarding it as merely a vehicle for librarians to redefine their roles in the digital age (Wilder, 2005).

The 2003 *Prague Declaration* (resulting form a UNESCO-sponsored conference) added weight to the importance of the concept regarding information literacy not only as an important set of skills to enable information to be gathered and used but also essential for effective participation in the 'information society', a basic human right and an integral part of education for all (USNCLIS, 2003). One of the basic principles within this document states,

---

[1] DfES The Future of Higher Education (2003), p44, and can be found at
http://www.dfes.gov.uk/hegateway/strategy/hestrategy/pdfs/DfES-HigherEducation.pdf

"The creation of an Information Society is key to social, cultural and economic development of nations and communities, institutions and individuals in the 21st century and beyond."

Building on the work done at Prague, the final report of the High-Level Colloquium on Information Literacy and Lifelong Learning held at Alexandria in November 2005 has recently been made available on the internet. In her press release announcing this publication Breivik (2006) says,

"The report argues that the existence of information holds little to no value to people who do not even know what information they need, much less whether it exists or not, or how to locate, evaluate and effectively use it."[2]

Breivik quotes Abdelaziz Abid, Senior Programme Specialist, Communications and Information Sector of UNESCO,

"Information literacy has become a global issue, and many Information Literacy initiatives are being documented throughout the world. Information Literacy forms the basis for lifelong learning. It is common to all disciplines, to all learning environments and to all levels of education".

It is generally recognised that information literacy teaching and learning requires a shift from teaching specific resources to a set of critical thinking skills involving the use of information (Kasowitz-Scheer & Pasqualoni, 2002). This is reflected in many current information literacy models and in recent research in information literacy teaching and learning (Bordinaro & Richardson, 2004). The most significant information literacy initiatives have taken place in the United States and Australia/ New Zealand (Virkus, 2003). There are also references to information literacy developments in specific countries such as, China, Japan, Mexico, Namibia, Singapore, South Africa (Virkus, 2003), Canada (Julien & Boon, 2002), Tanzania (Hepworth & Evans, 2006) and Turkey (Kirbanoglu, 2004). IFLA (the International Federation of Library Associations) is developing a definition (Lau, 2004) which is intended for application in any national context. Within the European Union (EU) a number of information literacy initiatives have been reported in local EU languages for example, Danish, Dutch, Finnish, French, German, Norwegian and Spanish amongst others (Virkus, 2003).

In the United Kingdom (UK) increased interest and activity in information literacy is reflected in the recent issues of the CILIP journal *Update* published in 2005 and 2006 which contained many articles entirely devoted to the

---

[2] Breivik, P. S., IFLANET press release March 6th 2006 and can be found at http://www.ifla.org/III/wsis/info-lit-for-all.htm

subject. Within the UK information literacy activity can be found in Higher Education (a recent example is Walton, 2005), Further Education (Arthur et al, 2005), the NHS (Brettle, 2003), schools (Smith & Hepworth, 2005) and the business sector (Lloyd, 2003). In Scotland information literacy has reached the political agenda via Dr John Crawford's petition to the Scottish Parliament (Webber, 2006).

There has been much debate regarding the terms *information* and *literacy* and the arguments for and against using these terms, whether they should be used together and what they mean (Owusu-Ansah, 2003). Again Australia and the United States have led the way in embracing and articulating the concept. In its Higher Education Competency Standards for 2000 the US based Association of College and Research Libraries (ACRL) defined information literacy as,

"an intellectual framework for understanding, finding, evaluating, and using information—activities which may be accomplished in part by fluency with information technology, in part by sound investigative methods, but most important, through critical discernment and reasoning".

According to their definition the information literate person must be,

"…able to recognize when information is needed and have the ability to locate, evaluate and use effectively the needed information"[3]

Across the world models have developed which characterize the skills and attributes an information literate person should have. In America there is the ACRL model, in Australia and New Zealand the Australian and New Zealand Institute for Information Literacy (ANZIIL) model and, closer to home in the United Kingdom, the Society of College, National and University Libraries (SCONUL) 7 pillars model (SCONUL, 1999), the Big Blue model created by the Joint Information Systems Committee (JISC) funded "Big Blue" project in 2002 and Chartered Institute of Library and Information Professionals (CILIP) contributed a new definition in 2005 (Armstrong et al 2005).

---

[3] *Information Literacy Competency Standards for Higher Education* by Association of College and Research Libraries (a division of the American Library Association), January 18, 2000. These standards were endorsed by the American Association for Higher Education and the Council of Independent Colleges in February, 2004.

Why is Information Literacy important now?

The external impetus
The massive increase in information available world wide is a huge imperative. In *Student learning in the information age* (1997) Breivik reports that the sum of human knowledge will double every 73 days by 2020. Terms such as 'information overload', 'data smog' and 'information glut' all capture the essence of the problem.

In the UK the gradual shift from a manufacturing industry to an information-based economy makes information literacy essential. The Government's agenda seems clear and later in 2006 the Leitch Review of Skills will report back to the HM Treasury on the optimum skills profile the UK should aim to achieve by 2020 in order to support productivity and economic growth as well as social objectives. The interim report was published in December 2005 and focused sharply on the need for functional numeracy and literacy. The Review is working with a wide range of stakeholders to build an evidence base in order to set ambitions for the second decade of the 21st century: the higher education sector needs to be ready to respond.

The higher education context: e-learning, PDP and the quality agenda
E-learning has become an increasing part of the higher education agenda (Stiles, 1999). Not only in the sense of the formal learning that takes place in classes and through VLEs, but also all the material that students use informally via the Internet, television and other media.

From 2006/7 the higher education sector will need to make provision for Personal Development Planning (QAA, 2000a) and institutions will have to provide an opportunity for students to record their learning experience formally and to show evidence of progression and higher learning. Information literacy skills can provide structure to students' reflective practice and enhance their learning.

The tracking of learning outcomes to match benchmarking statements made by the QAA (2000b) has encouraged higher education institutions to focus on information literacy. Subject benchmark statements for taught undergraduate subjects outline subject specific abilities and general transferable intellectual skills which reinforce the importance of students being information literate on graduation.

Indeed, information literacy lies at the heart of the QAA's definition of "graduateness". The QAA's "Understanding qualifications: the frameworks for higher education qualifications" web page describes honours level degrees in the following way,

"Honours level

Graduates with a bachelor's degree with honours will have developed an understanding of a complex body of knowledge, some of it at the current boundaries of an academic discipline. Through this, the graduate will have developed analytical techniques and problem-solving skills that can be applied in many types of employment. The graduate will be able to evaluate evidence, arguments and assumptions, to reach sound judgements, and to communicate effectively.

An honours graduate should have the qualities needed for employment in situations requiring the exercise of personal responsibility, and decision-making in complex and unpredictable circumstances."[4]

Now, more than ever, we need to ensure that these skills are acquired by students. From a librarian's or information professional's perspective, this is an excellent opportunity to work collaboratively with academic staff on an issue that is central to us all.

Information literacy: reviewing our position

In our view the challenge faced by information professionals and facilitators of learning is that there is a tendency, particularly amongst academic colleagues, to regard information literacy as mainly the development of IT skills rather than as an essential part of independent learning (Stubbings & Franklin, 2006). This is because information literacy's tools are regarded as largely technological but its field of interest encompasses the social and the personal (Whitworth, 2006). Initiatives such as Joint Information Systems Committee (JISC)'s re-packaging of information literacy within their i-skills agenda may reinforce this stereotypical view of information literacy as merely IT skills. However, it is clear that information literacy is part of a bigger picture; part of a jigsaw puzzle which includes other literacies (including for example, academic, media and digital), new ways of approaching learning through critical thinking, reflective practice, collaborative learning and the keyskills agenda all of which contribute to independent learning. Despite the fact that information literacy has many definitions, it is clear that these have common threads and give us the opportunity as information professionals to promote it as part of the learning agenda, rekindling our aspiration as educators and not just the keepers and organisers of information. Partnerships with the HEA and SCONUL take the information literacy agenda forward and the recent issue of ITALICS devoted to

---

[4] Quality Assurance Agency for Higher Education, (2000). Understanding qualifications: the frameworks for higher education qualifications:
http://www.qaa.ac.uk/students/guides/UnderstandQuals.asp (accessed 22/09/05)

information literacy initiatives (nationally and internationally) bear witness to this progress. We also believe that this conference demonstrates a sector wide commitment to information literacy.

Susie Andretta's paper aims to establish information literacy as the new 'pedagogy of the question' restating the view that information literacy is about 'learning how to learn' and cannot be separated from the learning process. Susie sees information literacy as a catalyst for educational change and suggests that the ability to learn independently is the appropriate response to the expanding information environment. She considers that information literacy is not just a library issue, but is also an educational and pedagogical issue, affecting academics and information professionals alike. Susie puts forward the view that an embedded approach is required to ensure that information literacy is fully integrated into curricula and that this approach should be supported by all those who are involved in its delivery. Susie believes that learners at the various stages of the learning continuum are not information literate; on the contrary they suffer from information overload and will operate according to entrenched spoon-feeding expectations. A self-discovery pedagogical model could reverse this trend: education needs to empower the learner.

Moira Bent's paper about the work being done at Newcastle University is heartening indeed. Writing with two academic colleagues she describes the efforts being made to build upon the SCONUL 7 pillars model to create a practical Toolkit with a pedagogical infrastructure. This Toolkit can be used a variety of ways to provide opportunities for the integration of information literacy into the curriculum. She outlines the steps being taken at Newcastle to develop a community of practice which equally involves information professionals, educationalists and subject academics. She explains the function of the University of Newcastle's Information Literacy Forum and describes its vitality, giving us a picture of a truly integrated partnership of colleagues working towards the institutional embedding of information literacy.

Rosie Jones and her colleagues at Manchester Metropolitan University have written a practical and instructive paper on the use of interactive white boards in support of information literacy sessions. They explain how the use of this new technology has been actively embraced by the information professionals at the University and how it seems to have boosted students' interest in such learning opportunities. Interactive white boards have already been used within primary and secondary teaching but their adoption has, it seems, been slower at tertiary level. This paper provides evidence of their positive use in an information literacy context.

The papers from Peter Godwin and from Tony Brauer look at the impact of easy internet searching and students' enchantment with this method of finding the information they need.

Peter's paper ponders what becomes of librarians and information professionals now that there are search engines and students really think they know how to use them effectively. How can information professionals sell their wares to the Net Generation? The Net Generation no longer wish to learn about libraries in an organisational context. Peter's paper puts forward useful ideas on how the SCONUL 7 pillars model can be used and developed so that the information literacy can still seems relevant to the seasoned Google searcher. Peter again emphasises the need to work in partnership and to cooperate with academic staff, especially where courses are moving to online modes of delivery. Information professionals must work to the adaptation of library systems rather than the adaptation of library users. Librarians must develop the confidence to teach information literacy in this context.

Tony Brauer has provided a paper which considers whether the keenness of students to adopt easy web searching using a variety of widely available search engines means that information professionals are witnessing a revolution in search patterns. Do narrow search terms mean that students are capturing specific data with little interpretive context and, if so, does this matter? How important is it for learners to contextualise and to evaluate research findings? Does using internet search engines help students and other researchers to do this, or, does their very presence mean that those looking for information begin to accept and indeed to seek only potentially conflicting and disparate data?

Sheila Webber and Bill Johnston give an insight into the strategic approach to information literacy within higher education. They discuss what might constitute an Information Literate University (ILU) and explain that this is the desired outcome for an institutional strategy within higher education. In reflecting on the potential aims, key leaders and stakeholders within an ILU Sheila and Bill draw on research which elicited academic colleagues' ideas about, and conceptions of, an ILU. They describe the early experience of being part of a Centre for Excellence in Teaching and Learning, namely the Centre for Inquiry-based Learning in the Arts and Social Sciences (CETL CILASS) at the University of Sheffield, which includes information literacy as a focus and they share observations of progress and practice in universities outside the UK. Sheila and Bill emphasise that information literacy is not just a library issue: it is a more fundamental issue of organisational culture and cannot rest on a "traditional" view but has to encompass this within a wide variety of channels and source types with an especially strong focus being on the using, sharing and communicating aspects of information literacy. The University of Sheffield's CETL CILASS, is used as an illustration of how to get information literacy onto institutional agendas. Sheila also shares some of the ideas about the stages in moving towards an ILU which she developed after working with librarians in Australia in 2002.

In his conclusion Mark Hepworth draws together the many strands that characterize information literacy in the higher education domain and suggests a synthesis and evaluation of the papers offered.

We hope you find this set of papers thought provoking and inspiring and that, if you were unable to attend the conference itself, it will give you a flavour of the day and its activities.

References

Andretta, S. (2005). Information Literacy: A Practitioners Guide. Oxford: Chandos.

Armstrong, C., Abell, A., Boden, D., Town, S. Webber, S. & Woolley, M. (2005). Defining Information Literacy for the UK. Update, vol. 4 (1-2), pp23 – 25.

Arthur, R., Stewart, C. & Irving, C. (2005). Bite-sized Learning for all Scottish Citizens. Update, vol. 4 (1-2), pp40 – 41.

Big Blue Project (2002). The Big Blue: Information Skills for Students: Final Report. [Online] http://www.leeds.ac.uk/bigblue/finalreport.html (accessed 31/7/2002).

Bordinaro, V. & Richardson, G. (2004). Scaffolding and Reflection in Course-Integrated Library Instruction. Journal of Academic Librarianship, vol. 30 (5), pp391-401.

Brettle, A. (2003). Information Skills Training: A Systematic Review. Health Information & Libraries Journal, vol 20 (Supp. 1) pp3-9.

Breivik, P. S. (1997). Student Learning in the Information Age. Phoenix: American Council on Education/Oryx Press Series on Higher Education.

Bruce, C. S. (1995). Information Literacy: a Framework for Higher Education. Australian Library Journal, August pp158-170.

Bundy, A. (2004). Australian and New Zealand Information Literacy Framework: Principles, Standards and Practice. Adelaide: Australian and New Zealand Institute for Information Literacy. [Online] http://www.anziil.org/resources/Info%20lit%202nd%20edition.pdf (accessed 8/2/2005)

Hepworth, M. & Evans, W. (2006). The design and implementation of an information literacy training course that integrated Information and Library Science conceptions of information literacy, educational theory and information behaviour research: a Tanzanian pilot study. ITALICS, 5 (1). [Online] http://www.ics.heacademy.ac.uk/italics/vol5iss1.htm (accessed 14/3/2006).

Julien, H. & Boon, S. (2002). From the Front Line: Information Literacy Instruction in Canadian Academic Libraries. Reference Services Review, vol. 30 (2), pp143-149.

Kasowitz-Scheer, A. & Pasqualoni, M. (2002). Information Literacy Instruction in Higher Education: Trends and Issues. ERIC DIGEST: ERIC Identifier: ED465375. [Online] http://www.ericdigests.org/2003-1/information.htm (Accessed 13/06/2005)

Kirbanoglu, S. S. (2004). An Overview of Information Literacy Studies in Turkey. International Information & Library Review, vol.36, pp23-27.

Lau, J. (2004). International Guidelines on Information Literacy. International Federation of Library Associations (IFLA). [Online] http://bivir/uacj.mex/dhi/DoctosNacioInter/Docs/Guidelines.pdf (accessed 13/08/2004).

Leitch, (2005). Leitch Review of Skills. Skills in the UK: The Long-Term Challenge. [Online] http://www.hm-treasury.gov.uk/media/1FE/8E/pbr05_leitchreviewexecsummary_255.pdf (accessed 1/03/2006).

Lloyd, A. (2003). Information Literacy: The Meta-competency of the Knowledge Economy? An Exploratory Paper. Journal of Librarianship and Information Science, vol. 32 (2), pp87-92.

Owusu-Ansah (2003). Information Literacy and the Academic Library: A Critical Look at the Concept and the Controversies Surrounding it. Journal of Academic Librarianship, vol. 29 (4), pp219-230.

Quality Assurance Agency for Higher Education (2000a). Guidelines for HE Progress Files. [Online] http://www.qaa.ac.uk/academicinfrastructure/progressFiles/guidelines/progfile2001.asp (accessed 22/2/06)

Quality Assurance Agency for Higher Education (2000b). Honours Degree Benchmark statements. [Online] http://www.qaa.ac.uk/academicinfrastructure/benchmark/honours/default.asp (accessed 22/09/05)

Smith, M. & Hepworth, M. (2005). Motivating Learners to become Information Literate. Update, vol. 4 (1–2), pp46-47.

Society of College, National & University Libraries (SCONUL): Advisory Committee on Information Literacy (1999). Information Skills in Higher Education: A SCONUL Position Paper. [Online] http://www.sconul.ac.uk/activities/inf_lit/papers/Seven_pillars2.pdf (accessed 16/4/2002).

Stiles, M. (1999). Effective Learning and the Virtual Learning Environment. [Online] http://www.staffs.ac.uk/COSE/cose10/posnan.html (accessed 22/2/06).

Stubbings, R. & Franklin, G. (2006). Does Advocacy help to embed Information Literacy into the Curriculum? A Case Study. ITALICS, 5 (1). [Online] http://www.ics.heacademy.ac.uk/italics/vol5iss1.htm (accessed 14/3/2006).

United States National Commission on Library and Information Science (USNCLS) (2003). The Prague Declaration. Towards an Information Literate Society. [Online] http://www.nclis.gov/libinter/infolitconf&meet/post-infolitconf&meet/PragueDeclaration.pdf (accessed 23/3/2005).

Virkus, S. (2003). Information Literacy in Europe: A Literature Review. Information Research, vol. 8 (4). [Online] http://informationr.net/ir/8-4/paper159.html (Accessed 27/06/2005).

Walton, G. (2005). Assessing Students is Essential for Success. Update, vol. 4 (1–2), pp36-37.

Webber, S. (2006). Information Literacy Weblog: Information Literacy Petition to Scottish Parliament: Update. [Online] http://information-literacy.blogspot.com/2006/01/information-literacy-petition-to.html (accessed 5/4/2006).

Wilder, S. (2005). Information Literacy Makes all the Wrong Assumptions. Chronicle Review, vol. 51, January 7. [Online] http://www.bright.net/~dlackey/WrongAssumptions.htm (accessed 24/05/2005).

Whitworth, A. (2006). Communicative Competence in the Information Age: Towards a Critical Theory of Information literacy Education. ITALICS, 5 (1). [Online] http://www.ics.heacademy.ac.uk/italics/vol5iss1.htm (accessed 14/3/2006).

Information Literacy: the new "pedagogy of the question"?

Susie Andretta - School of Information Management, London Metropolitan University

Abstract

The paper aims to establish information literacy as the new pedagogy of the question reiterating the view that information literacy is about 'learning how to learn' and that, because of this, it cannot be separated from the learning process (Lupton, 2004), but should be used as a catalyst for educational change (Bruce, 2002). We shall examine a number of premises that lead to this conclusion. First the ability for independent learning is the appropriate response to a constantly expanding information environment. This is in contrast with the view that learning is about the accumulation of static knowledge (Marton, 1981). Secondly information literacy is not just a library issue, but is also an educational and pedagogical issue that affects academics and information professionals alike. It follows from this that an embedded approach is required to ensure that information literacy is fully integrated into curricula and supported by all those who are involved in its delivery. Thirdly learners at the various stages of the learning continuum are not information literate, on the contrary they suffer from information overload and operate according to deeply entrenched spoon-feeding expectations (Andretta, 2005). Fourthly the learning culture of HE institutions reinforces the spoon-feeding expectations of students by promoting a transmittal mode of delivery that prioritises regular face-to-face attendance rather than encouraging the self-discovery pedagogical model. That education needs to empower and not domesticate (Bundy, 2004) is the dominant theme of this paper which will be illustrated at the conference through examples of information literacy practice at London Metropolitan University and through students' experiences of the learn-how-to-learn approach.

Introduction

The paper promotes the view that there is a parallel between information literacy as a way of emancipating the learner through the development of independent and lifelong learning and the "pedagogy of the question" devised by Paulo Freire to describe a critical pedagogy which gives the learner control over the learning process. This type of emancipation raises issues of control over the curriculum which inevitably associate information literacy with contentious power relations within HE. Evidence shows that information literacy provision can be resisted by library and faculty staff who perceive it as challenging their professional practice. On the other hand, those who do embrace the pedagogy of the question may face institutional hostility that, in extreme cases such as the one presented here, result in the dismissal of such practice, despite clear evidence that this approach is welcomed by, and beneficial to the students.

Empowering the learner through the pedagogy of the question

The dominant themes of this paper are that education needs to empower and not domesticate (Bundy, 2005), and that the emancipation of the learner can be achieved by the learn-how-to-learn approach advocated by information literacy (Andriella, 2006). Independent learning as a primary educational aim is not a recent phenomenon, as shown by Robinson's call over a century ago, for librarians to become facilitators of students' self-reliant learning. The emphasis here is on lifelong learning that goes beyond the taught investigation of the disciplines.

> [..] a librarian should be more than a keeper of books; he should be an educator [..] All that is taught in college amounts to very little; but if we can send students out self-reliant in their investigations, we have accomplished very much. (Robinson cited in Lantz & Brage, 2006)

Making learners capable of independent and lifelong learning requires a critical pedagogy (Whitworth, 2006) whose empowering effect is captured by Freire's theory of the pedagogy of the question, which he defines as:

> [...] a practice that forces and challenges the learners to think critically and to adopt a critical attitude toward the world [...] Unlike the pedagogy of the answer, which reduces learners to mere receptacles for prepackaged knowledge, the pedagogy of the question gives learners the 'language of possibility' to challenge the every constraints which relegate them to mere objects [...] We teach biology, philosophy, linguistics, etc. When we meet the students, we start giving answers to them without listening to their questions. This is what I call a 'pedagogy of answers' instead of pedagogy of questions. (Bruss and Macedo, 1985: 8-9)

Similar arguments are put forward by information literacy promoters such as Bundy (2004) who states that to address the challenges of an information rich society students need to learn to identify pathways to knowledge and focus on the questions that rarely change, rather than on the answers which continually change. In addition, Bruce's relational model (1997) emphasises an holistic evaluation of people's experience of information literacy and learning. The latter is defined as a qualitative change in the way the learner conceptualises phenomena in the real world, rather than measuring the amount of discipline-specific knowledge, or the level of skills reached. Recent collaborative research by Bruce, Edwards and Lupton (2006), on the *Six Frames for Information literacy Education* endorses the relational model as one of these frames and promotes a learning that is based on the principles of discernment and variation. In other words, a process that focuses on a qualitative change in learners' awareness, rather than the measurement of skills and knowledge (Marton and Booth, 1997). A full exploration of the Six Frames goes beyond the scope of this paper, and can be found in Andretta (2006b).

Freire argues that the shift towards a pedagogy of the question requires educators to let go of disciplinary certainties and learn to deal with the tension between silence and voice, as this defines the educator-student relationship.

> The question for me as a teacher is not just to become silent now and say bureaucratically to the students that it is time for you to speak (because it is written in the curriculum). What I have to do is learn how to challenge students to [..] find their voices, to get [..] into speech [..] into concreteness, and little by little I also have to go into silence [..] (Bruss and Macedo, 1985: 16)

By being aware of the tension between silence and voice educators encourage learners to find their own voice and their own unique way of learning. These processes generate a sense of ownership of learning, what Fazey and Marton describe as making what is learned 'your own' (2002: 235), and a consequent transformation of the learner resulting in the learner's internalisation of the information (Bruce, 1997; Lupton, 2004; Edwards, 2006; Bruce et al, 2006). The information literacy undergraduate module at the Department of Applied Social Sciences, London Metropolitan University offers a good example of students' empowerment by fostering their competence in expressing and sharing ideas, in Freire's words they find their voice.

> As well as learning new things that are really useful to my coursework I get to express my views or listen to other people's thoughts on the subjects [...] and getting the teacher's opinion too. This way it's easier to learn and understand the subject more than just reading about it.[5]

In addition, the module's role as the Higher Education Orientation (HEO) module (one of the core requirements of the University-wide undergraduate scheme) makes it imperative that students are equipped with the necessary confidence to operate effectively in an often unfamiliar HE environment. This confidence is developed by making the students responsible for their own level of engagement and a consequent progression as information literate and

---

[5] Extract from a student's self-assessment task.

independent learners. The pedagogical rationale supporting this approach is based on two separate, but similar perspectives. The first one is illustrated by Freire's idea that educators need to take into account students' wisdom and encourage them to voice it (Bruss and Macedo, 1985: 10), and the second one is found in Marton's view (1981) that learning is influenced by how learners relate to what they are learning and how they use the knowledge they already possess. To ascertain the students' information literacy attitudes at the start of the module, they are asked to complete a web-based diagnostic questionnaire with the aim of producing a learning profile customised to reflect the learning needs of each student. On the basis of this feedback students assess their initial strengths and weaknesses in information literacy, and this self-evaluation process informs their decision on whether to attend the class-based activities or complete the module remotely. Those who encounter difficulties in between classes can also take advantage of tutorial support available online. Again, a full account of the information litaracy module cannot be included in this paper, but is available as a case study in Andretta (2005). Here we explore the impact of voluntary attendance on the students' motivation, and most importantly on their development as responsible learners. The feedback is taken from the written self-evaluation report, part of the assessed portfolio, where students are asked, amongst other things, to comment on whether they found non-compulsory attendance beneficial or not and why.

Overall the students respond positively to the flexibility offered by the learn-how-to-learn approach promoted by the information literacy module, and welcome the opportunity to choose how to engage with the learning resources and the assessment tasks according to the mode of study that best suits their needs and circumstances. Not surprisingly they list a number of empowering effects when taking responsibility for their studies, including the establishment of a more equal relationship between tutor and students, one based on the belief that students can and want to actively engage with the learning process, but must be encouraged to do so at their own pace. This is what Freire refers to when he exhorts educators to acknowledge the wisdom of their students (Bruss and Macedo, 1985: 10).

> [...] non-compulsory attendance increases the trust between the pupil and the tutor. I feel that tutors often think you do little or no work because you have not attended the lectures, but this module proves overwise.[6]

Some students also comment favourably about the flexibility of information literacy provision underpinned by a support framework that fosters

---

[6] Extract from a student's self-assessment task.

independent, but at the same time supported learning, and which frees students' time for other commitments.

It encourages individuals to be in control and take responsibility for their education. As a part time evening student with a child I found this very useful as it meant that I didn't have to attend [all the] lectures. The module is structured in such an effective way that one can do the assessments away from class and fit them in around their busy lifestyle [..]. This allowed me to spend valuable time with my daughter.[7]

In addition, other students appreciate the availability of a wide range of learning resources and the step-by-step familiarisation with independent learning and academic literacy required to progress in their studies. This, they claim, leads to improved self-discipline and the ability to manage their time more effectively, but more importantly it enables them to test and develop their confidence as independent learners who take control of how and what to learn.

Independent learning gives students the opportunity to be able to work at their own pace, yet know that all the support systems are in place [..] this way students can get the help and advice in the areas that they need, yet work on their own at home if they feel confident enough to carry out the allocated tasks.[8]

Giving students a choice of how to engage with the learning process increases their sense of control over the pace of learning and, at the same time, keeps them motivated and challenged by making the learning relevant to their needs.

I learnt what I needed to at my own pace, rather than learning something new each week at the lectures and not fully understanding what was taught, then having to catch up with those more experienced [..] This method also ensured that I kept interested as well as challenged.[9]

Even those who express a negative disposition towards the principles of independent learning and information literacy raise some interesting examples of students who have learned a valuable and timely lesson at an early stage of their academic career which prepares them for independent study at advanced level. Whilst they complain that lack of compulsion demotivates them and results in a falling behind with the work, nevertheless there is a final realisation of the importance of managing the workload effectively and the resolution of applying this strategy to future practices.

I found I had a lack of motivation to go to the lectures [..]. Therefore, I found it hard to keep up with the work when it was supposed to be completed and this resulted in my falling behind and having work pile up

---

[7] Extract from a student's self-assessment task.
[8] Extract from a student's self-assessment task.
[9] Extract from a student's self-assessment task.

[..].However, I have learnt now to keep on top of the work and to complete it when it is first given to me instead of leaving it to the last minute.[10]

Information literacy, a profound educational issue

If we define information literacy in terms of independent learning and associate it with the pedagogy of the question, as is the intention of this paper, then the process of making students information literate becomes an educational issue, rather than the sole responsibility of the library (Bundy 1997; Snavely, 2001). Evidence shows that the classification of information literacy as a pedagogical concern raises issues of power and control over the curriculum that cause tension at various levels of provision. For example, promoting information literacy as the learning-how-to-learn approach requires some librarians to adjust their perspectives and perceive this phenomenon in terms of a more dynamic and holistic process of information use rather than as mechanistic information seeking practices. "For librarians who base their information literacy programs on technology, sources, process and control, it is a challenge to think beyond information seeking." (Lupton 2004: 80) On the other hand, when librarians begin to assume the role of information literacy educators, faculty staff perceive this development as an infringement of their academic territory and respond by resisting attempts of collaboration with library staff. (Bundy, 2004; Stubbings & Franklin, 2006)

Information literacy practice that fosters a pedagogy of the question also carries the risk of alienating tutors operating within institutions that insist on promoting a pedagogy of the answer. In some extreme cases this generates conditions where educators are divested of the opportunity to continue teaching (Bruss and Macedo, 1985: 12). The withdrawal of the information literacy module at London Metropolitan University is a case in point, where the aim of making students independent learners is dismissed in favour of a policy of regular face-to-face attendance in the core provision of the undergraduate scheme. A full account of the challenges faced by the information literacy module is given elsewhere (Andretta, 2005b). Here we explore the rationale underpinning the University's decision to drop the module to illustrate evidence of institutional resistance against the pedagogy of the question. The main argument rests on the belief that the HEO module is the place where the HE environment is made less intimidating to students and that this level of familiarisation can only be achieved through face-to-face delivery. Any deviation from this position sends the wrong signals because it undermines the principle of building a physical interaction with the students which is the University's primary aim at first year undergraduate level. Independent learning

---

[10] Extract from a student's self-assessment task.

is regarded as something to be dealt with further down the road after the students have become familiar with the HE environment. In practice, the University's view that first year undergraduate students are not mature enough to operate as effective independent learners and like scared children they need to be reassured solely through face-to-face contact is challenged by the students' claims that the independent learning enhances their control over the process and pace of learning, and their need to be acknowledged by tutors and by the University as mature and responsible learners.

In addition, over-reliance on face-to-face delivery only reinforces the spoon-feeding expectations of academically weak students. This problem is compounded by the fact that learners at various stages of the learning continuum are not information literate; on the contrary they suffer from information overload and operate according to deeply entrenched spoon-feeding expectations (Andretta, 2005). Therefore, the pursuit of independent learning is resented and resisted by these students who experience the anxiety of having to come to terms with such an unfamiliar learning approach. However, the fact that students are not information literate or familiar with HE from the outset only strengthens the need to introduce them to the learning-how-to-learn approach during the first year of their studies to ensure that they develop the required confidence to perform as independent learners when they reach advanced level work.

From institutions for teaching to institutions of learning?

The paper has presented examples of diverse challenges encountered by information literacy as the 'new' pedagogy of the question. These are depicted in the literature as strong resistance from faculty and library staff who experience the shifting to this type of pedagogy as a threat to their professional identity. On the other hand, those who enthusiastically promote this pedagogy run the risk of having their practice curtailed simply because it challenges the appropriateness of institutional learning and teaching policies. What causes most concern about these institutional practices is that policy makers, who have little knowledge of students' learning profiles, can impose learning and teaching strategies that are out of touch with the students' educational requirements, thus preventing them from developing into independent and lifelong learners. Bundy comments that the progress towards the establishment of institutions of learning through the implementation of information literacy education and the pedagogy of the question is slow and uneven (2004: 8). However in some extreme cases, progress is not just slow but reversed back to an authoritarian pedagogy of the answer which results in the disempowerment of students and tutors, as both are denied a voice.

References

Andretta, S. (2006b in press) Phenomenography a conceptual framework for information literacy, Aslib Proceedings New information perspectives.

Andretta, S. (2006) Information Literacy: challenges of implementation, ITALICS, 5(1). [Online] Available at: http://www.ics.heacademy.ac.uk/italics/vol5iss1.htm (Accessed: 10 March 2006)

Andretta, S. (2005b) Information literacy: empowering the learner "against all odds". LILAC 2005: Librarians' Information Literacy Annual Conference. April 4-6 2005, Imperial College, London. [Online] Available at Tangentium, May 2005: http://www.personal.leeds.ac.uk/%7Epolaw/tangentium/may05/feature3.html

Andretta, S. (2005) Information Literacy: a practitioner's guide. Oxford: Chandos Publishing.

Bruce, C. & Edwards, S. L. & Lupton, M. (2006) Six Frames for Information literacy Education: a conceptual framework for interpreting the relationships between theory and practice, in Andretta, S. (ed), Italics, 5 (1), January 2006. [Online]. Available at: http://www.ics.heacademy.ac.uk/italics/vol5iss1.htm (Accessed: 16 January 2006).

Bruce C. (1997) The Seven Faces of Information Literacy. Adelaide: Auslib Press.

Bruss, N. and Macedo, D.P. (1985) "Toward a Pedagogy of the Question: Conversations with Paulo Freire." , Journal of Education, 167(2): 7-21.

Bundy, A. (2005) Changing and connecting the educational silos: the potential of the information literacy framework. LILAC 2005: Librarians' Information Literacy Annual Conference. April 4-6 2005, Imperial College, London.

Bundy, A. (2004) Zeitgeist*: information literacy and educational change. Paper presented at the 4th Frankfurt Scientific Symposium, Germany, October 4, 2004. Available at: http://www.library.unisa.edu.au/about/papers/abpapers.asp. (Accessed, 16 January 2006)

Bundy, A. (1997) Pedagogy, Politics, Power: Preaching Information Literacy to the unconverted. Keynote address of Information Literacy the Catholic Teacher Librarians Conference in New South Wales, 3 August 1997.

Edwards, S. (in press 2006) 'Follow the yellow brick road' Information literacy: an evidence based approach. Australian and New Zealand Institute for Information Literacy. Adelaide: Auslib Press.

Fazey, J. & Marton, F. (2002) Understanding the space of experiential variation, Active Learning in higher education, 3(3): 234-250.

Lantz, A. and Brage, C. (2006) Towards a Learning Society – Exploring the Challenge of Applied Information Literacy through Reality-Based Scenarios, in Andretta, S. (ed), Italics, 5 (1), January 2006. [Online]. Available at: http://www.ics.heacademy.ac.uk/italics/vol5iss1.htm (Accessed: 16 January 2006).

Lupton, M. (2004) The Learning Connection. Information Literacy and the student experience, Auslib Press, Adelaide.

Marton, F. (1981) Phenomenography - Describing conceptions of the world around us, Instructional Science, 10: 177-200. [Online]. Available at: http://www.ped.gu.se/biorn/phgraph/misc/constr/phegraph.html (Accessed: 16 January 2006)

Marton, F. & Booth, S. (1997) Learning and Awareness, Mahwah, New Jersey, LEA

Snavely, L. (2001) Information Literacy Standards for Higher Education: An International Perspective, 67th IFLA Council and General Conference Libraries and Librarians: Making a Difference in the Knowledge Age, Boston, USA, 16-21 August 2001: 1-4.

Whitworth, A. (2006) Communicative competence in the information age: Towards a critical theory of information literacy education. ITALICS, 5(1). [Online] Available at: http://www.ics.heacademy.ac.uk/italics/vol5iss1.htm (Accessed: 10 March 2006)

Developing a Community of Practice:
The Newcastle Information Literacy Project

Moira Bent - Robinson Library, University of Newcastle upon Tyne
Steve Higgins - School of Education, University of Newcastle upon Tyne
Sophie Brettell - Quality in Teaching & Learning, University of Newcastle upon Tyne.

Introduction

"What are people thinking of when we talk about information literacy?"(Moore, 2002)
At Newcastle we felt that some, even though they may be information literate themselves, were thinking of information literacy as a skill, rather than as an essential element in learning. (Merchant and Hepworth, 2002, Webber et al., 2005). Even now, information literacy is not addressed in many librarianship courses (Weller, 2006) and hardly at all in teacher training or academic practice courses (Wilson, 1997). This Project attempts to engage academic and library staff more deeply with the concepts and processes of information literacy, rather than the products. "Information literacy demands a different way of thinking about what and how we teach as well as thinking about the impact on learning" (Moore, 2002). Kuhlthau (1996) also emphasises the importance of students understanding the process rather than just finding a result. We want to engage staff in providing active and explicit experiences in which students explore aspects of information literacy and develop both their information literacy and effective learning habits or dispositions (Claxton and Carr, 2004). The rationale for this approach draws on a number of theories, particularly the development of self-regulated learning (Zeidner et al., 2000) and at staff level, activity theory (Tuomi-Gröhn and Engeström, 2003) with its valuable notion of boundary crossing as a means to achieve transfer of learning. The project outcome will therefore be a fuzzy collection of ideas, approaches and examples that take into account a range of approaches to learning (see, for example Vermunt's (2005) overview) and teaching methods.

Methodology

Begun in summer 2005, the project has the specific purpose of "providing Schools with a suite (toolkit) of interactive learning activities relating to information literacy that can be integrated seamlessly with curricular provision…. it is proposed to embed information literacy development firmly on the learning agenda, the Library working in partnership with Academic Schools, the Centre for Academic Development and the Staff Development Unit" (Bent, 2005) The benefits of the project were to be that " the Library will have a demonstrably coherent approach to the delivery of IL across the curriculum to all levels, the project will create a learning environment in which students will develop life-long and transferable IL habits... academic staff will have available a mechanism by which they can integrate IL into their teaching" (Bent 2005).

The project team includes academics, librarians and educationalists. As well as providing essential expertise this mix contributes to the perception of the project as a university initiative, rather than as 'just another library project'.

Pick and Mix approach

The Toolkit is based on the Sconul 7 pillars model (SCONUL, 1999), setting benchmarks for information literacy development through university life. Work at South Bank University (Godwin, 2003) has informed this development. Each pillar is divided into sub-topics that have been mapped to a range of activities designed to appeal to different learning attitudes and teaching situations, thus providing pick and mix opportunities for staff. For example, plagiarism activities include slides, ideas for group work, handouts, an online tutorial produced by staff in the Medical School, links to external tutorials, Blackboard quizzes with extensive feedback, examples of plagiarism in the news and examples of best practice, as well as suggestions for further reading. Suggested activity selections will be provided for each faculty, giving staff a contextualised demonstration of how to build sets of activities into modules and across programmes to ensure all 7 pillars are covered. We believe this practical and pragmatic approach will be crucial to the success of the toolkit. We have been influenced by Bruce Ingraham's work on readability (Ingraham, 2004) and are currently wrestling with the need to ensure that the Toolkit is transparent and usable for staff whilst at the same time maintaining its complexity. Versions of the Toolkit will be available on the Information Literacy website (Newcastle University Library, 2005) from summer 2006.

Development through process – the Information Literacy Forum

The Toolkit is the anticipated product of the project, but the process itself has engendered a much more interesting outcome - the Information Literacy Forum. The Forum was initiated as a consultation vehicle to discover more about academic attitudes to information literacy and their priorities for activities in the Toolkit. Feedback from the Forum indicated that as well as providing this data, lecturers involved had found it a useful networking opportunity; contacts had been made with colleagues in other disciplines, discussions on the different approaches to information literacy had provided much food for thought. Some staff, unable to come to the meeting, still registered an interest and so the online Forum was born! It allows staff to register both interest and involvement in information literacy by submitting details to a secure database.

It is supported by email discussion as well as meetings and we have been encouraged by the interest shown. Engagement by staff is illustrated by this email sent by a senior lecturer in Computing Science to his colleagues:
"I ran into Moira this morning .. mentioned the fact that we had been influenced by the discussion about information literacy to include more background reading and research into the literature into some of our modules. .....I would be interested in strengthening critical evaluation, also in seeing if we can make the benefits of reading the literature more apparent to the students (through coursework, primarily). Some CSCxxx students have definitely got some of this - a few have remarked, for example, on the lack of hard science in the literature on UML 2.0. In trying to set the CSCxxx exam (it's a struggle!) I realise there's an effect on assessment - can we dare ask for critical evaluation of claims in the software engineering literature in an exam, or do we stick to good old "prove the following" questions)?." (Fitzgerald, 2005)
Other academics are also engaging with information literacy (a University Teaching Fellowship to embed IL into the Chemistry curriculum, an English Subject Centre grant to develop tools for writing support in English, projects in Environmental Science and Computing, links with an FDTL5 project in Education) and we are using the Forum as a mechanism to share experiences and good practice from these initiatives.

Pedagogical infrastructure

A key feature of the Toolkit is its underpinning pedagogical approach. Developing appropriate pedagogies for information literacy is recognised as a key issue (Leckie and Fullerton, 1998, Webber and Johnston, 2002). The Toolkit supports integration and development of information literacy activities at three broad educational levels. At the first level it provides activities which can be delivered by library staff or used independently by learners. At the second level these resources are available for tutors, in collaboration with library staff, to integrate into course materials. It is anticipated that this will be the most effective approach. This will be the key to pedagogical development as the integration of information literacy requires understanding from both subject and information perspectives. As this understanding deepens over time it should enrich curriculum development outside information literacy. At the third level the Forum acts as a development group, or community of practice (Wenger, 1998), where the development of information literacy provides the joint enterprise for the development of a shared repertoire of resources. This is a pragmatic approach, based on development work on thinking skills in schools (Leat and Higgins, 2002), and recognises that staff will engage with the Forum at different times and at different levels, but that the continuum represented by these three broad levels offers opportunities for staff to become more involved and engaged.

Institutional embedding

Effective integration and embedding of information literacy at the institutional level is unlikely to be sustained unless staff are involved in an active process of development (Bruce, 2001); it is hoped that the Forum will support this, providing a catalyst for educational change (Bruce, 2002). However, so far we have still only talked to a small proportion of staff, so to discover other practice taking place we are actively seeking alternative ways of reaching across the institution.

The inclusion of information literacy as a skills outcome on all university module outline forms was discussed at our last Forum. Analysis of the forms enables us to target staff who claim to assess or practice information literacy in their modules and to analyse which Schools seem most active in this respect. 135 modules include information literacy in their learning outcomes and the modules are fairly evenly distributed across Faculty and Degree type. Skills are being assessed without being introduced or practiced, and/or practiced without ever being assessed. Interestingly, these modules do not correlate directly with the modules taught by staff attending the forum. We are in the process of mapping the outcomes for these information literacy-inclusive modules onto the Toolkit and once this is complete will approach the teaching staff with suggestions for activities that could support the outcomes and/or with an offer to help them rearticulate the outcomes. We hope that this very practical approach will be one of the ways in which we will encourage more staff to join the Forum. The addition of information literacy to student Personal Development Plans this year may also aid the process of embedding at institutional level, as observed at Loughborough (Stubbings and Franklin, 2006). The university is in the process of revising its Key Skills Framework and information literacy is being included as essential for the first time. This institutional level support bolsters the work being done with individual academic staff.

Conclusion

Whilst the initial project had a purely pragmatic aim, the pedagogical infrastructure of the toolkit validates and confirms the educational value of the activities. The community of practice growing through the Forum contributes to the integration of information literacy at institutional level. This takes the focus away from the library and situates it firmly on the mainstream teaching agenda. A natural extension to the work will be to study the use of the Toolkit once it has been launched, facilitate subject embedding and to develop a dimension relating to assessment and the measure of attainment.

References

Bent, M. (2005) Information Literacy Project : Project Definition Statement. Robinson Library, University of Newcastle

Bruce, C. S. (2001) Faculty librarian partnerships in Australian higher education, critical dimensions Reference Services Review, 29, 2

Bruce, C. S. (2002) Information Literacy as a Catalyst for Educational Change: A Background Paper: White Paper prepared for UNESCO, the U.S. National Commission on Libraries and Information Science, and the National Forum on Information Literacy, for use at the Information Literacy Meeting of Experts, Prague, The Czech Republic. http://www.nclis.gov/libinter/infolitconf&meet/papers/bruce-fullpaper.pdf

Claxton, G. and Carr, M. A. (2004) A framework for teaching learning: the dynamics of disposition Early Years, 24, 87-97

Fitzgerald, J. (2005) Information Literacy and CSC, personal email, 17.11.05.

Godwin, P. (2003) 'Information Literacy, but at what level?' in Martin, A. and Rader, H.(Eds) Information and IT Literacy: enabling learning in the 21st century. Facet: London, pp. 88-97.

Ingraham, B. (2004) Guidelines for producing Readable, Accessible Onscreen text BB Matters.http://www.bbmatters.net/bbmattersProject/Articles/article_item.asp?SubmitArticleID=67

Kuhlthau, C. C. (1996) 'The process of learning from information', in Kuhlthau, C. C.(Ed), The Virtual School Library. Gateway to the Information Superhighway. Libraries Unlimited Inc: Eaglewood, pp. 95-103.

Leat, D. and Higgins, S. (2002) The role of powerful pedagogical strategies in curriculum development . The Curriculum Journal, 13, 1 71-85

Leckie, G. J. and Fullerton, A. (1998) The Roles of Academic Librarians in Fostering a Pedagogy for Information Literacy: Proceedings of the 9th Association of College and Research Libraries National Conference. http://www.ala.org/ala/acrl/acrlevents/leckie99.pdf

Merchant, L. and Hepworth, M. (2002) Information literacy of teachers and pupils in secondary schools Journal of Librarianship and Information Science, 34, 2 81-89

Moore, P. (2002) Information Literacy, what's it all about? New Zealand Council for Educational Research: Wellington.

Newcastle University Library (2005) The Newcastle Information Literacy Forum website. Available at: http://www.ncl.ac.uk/library/infolit.php (Accessed: 23.2.06).

SCONUL (1999) Information skills in Higher Education : a Sconul position paper prepared by the Sconul Advisory Committee on Information Literacy. Society of College, National and University Libraries.

Stubbings, R. and Franklin, G. (2006) Does advocacy help to embed information literacy into the curriculum? A case study ITALICS, 5, 1.http://www.ics.heacademy.ac.uk/italics/vol5iss1.htm

Tuomi-Gröhn, T. and Engeström, Y. (Eds). (2003) Between school and work: New perspectives on transfer and boundary-crossing. Pergamon Press, Amsterdam.

Vermunt, J. D. (2005) Relations between student learning patterns and personal and contextual factors and academic performance Higher Education, 49, 205 234

Webber, S., Boon, S. and Johnston, B. (2005) UK academics' conceptions of, and pedagogy for, information literacy : presentation at LILAC, 2005.: LILAC : Librarian's Information Literacy Annual Conference. London,

Webber, S. and Johnston, B. (2002) Conceptions of information literacy: New perspectives and implications Journal of Information Science, 26, 6 381-397.http://search.epnet.com/login.aspx?direct=true&db=buh&an=3966518

Weller, K. (2006) Putting our own house in order Library and Information Update, 5, 1-2 30-32

Wenger, E. (1998) Communities of practice. Learning meaning and identity. CUP: Cambridge.

Wilson, K. (1997) 'Information skills: the reflections and perceptions of student teachers and related professionals', in Lighthall, L.(Ed), Information Rich but Knowledge Poor? Emerging Issues for Schools and Libraries Worldwide. International Association of School Librarianship, Seattle, WA, pp. 63-74.

Zeidner, M., Boekarts, M. and Pintrich, P. R. (2000) 'Self-regulation:Directions and challenges for future research', in Boekaerts, M., Pintrich, P. and Zeidner, M.(Eds) Self-regulation: Theory, research, and applications. Academic Press: Orlando, FL, pp. 749-768

Providing for the next generation: adopting interactive whiteboards in information literacy training.

Rosie Jones, Karen Peters , Emily Shields
InfoSkills team, Manchester Metropolitan University

The importance of Information Literacy (IL) training has long been asserted in library literature. However, convincing students that they need such training remains a challenge. Research has shown that one way of demonstrating the relevance of IL is to embed it within students' courses and assessments. Yet in order for training to be effective, it is also crucial that students are engaged in the classroom and that they enjoy the learning experience. The Manchester Metropolitan University (MMU) Library InfoSkills team, established in June 2005, coordinates IL training across the library service and aims to ensure that the programme is delivered as effectively as possible. As part of this mandate, the team is currently investigating strategies for integrating new technologies into classroom teaching sessions as a means of enhancing the student learning experience through engaging and interactive IL delivery. This paper will focus on the use of Interactive Whiteboards (IWBs) in IL training and the success in adopting this new technology at MMU Library.

The adoption of IWBs as a teaching aid has been extensive in UK schools, but in higher education (HE) this implementation has not been so widespread, with the main usage being in teacher training departments (Becta, 2003; TechLearn, no date). Little has been written regarding the use of IWBs in HE. Although their installation at MMU has been extensive and they form part of the standard kit in MMU's technology-enhanced teaching rooms, in the majority of cases they are used merely as glorified projection screens. Yet, according to JISC: "Studies have found [IWBs] to be highly motivating and learner-centred when integrated innovatively. They offer a powerful facility for integrating media elements into teaching to enhance content and support collaborative learning" (TechLearn, no date, p.6). As an increasing number of schools adopt whiteboard technology, there is a growing possibility that students arriving in HE have been taught with them. Hence, with greater student expectations and the potential for IWBs to transform teaching, by making it interactive, visual and motivating, IWB uptake in HE is crucial.

The MMU Library Service quickly recognised the importance of IWBs in terms of IL training and was keen to integrate this technology into its teaching. This has been highlighted by the purchase of IWBs for each of MMU's seven site libraries. There are two key reasons for the library's rapid response to this technology. Firstly, research shows that "learning is optimal when it is an active process" (Philip and Schmidt, 2004); IWBs provide an easy form of interactivity which should stimulate and engage an audience. Secondly, adopting and using IWBs to their full potential allows the library to not only enhance training experiences but also to impress both the student and the academic. They have seen that the library is at the forefront of technology adoption and this in turn has raised the profile and the status of the library in the university. The IWB has the ability to transform IL training at MMU Library even further, whilst establishing the library as forerunners in this new teaching development within the academic community.

IWBs have changed InfoSkills provision greatly as they have allowed a level of participation in training sessions that was not previously possible. Used in conjunction with the specialist software (ACTIVstudio 2)[11] they allow trainers to pre-prepare flipcharts (similar to PowerPoint slides) or to annotate over any application that is currently running. MMU Library is also piloting an audience participation voting system (ACTIVote)[1] as part of this software which allows the trainer to conduct votes throughout the session. This keeps the event interactive and allows the trainer to assess if key concepts have been understood by the audience. Perhaps most importantly, research has shown that IWBs are able to support a range of learning styles and intelligences (Promethean Ltd., 2004) which is the fundamental aim of any successful training session.

ACTIVstudio functions have been utilised in MMU InfoSkills sessions in the following ways:
- Using flipcharts to write up keywords from a search query, allowing interaction as students shout out the answers.
- Highlighting areas in a PowerPoint presentation or on a website.
- Using the timer facility to ensure that set exercises run to time.
- Using ACTIVote for knowledge checks and evaluation.
- Using ACTIVote to break up lectures and engage the audience.

Since IWBs have been used in InfoSkills sessions the benefits to the Library and the students have been sizeable. Library staff are conscious that the sessions they are running are far more interesting and interactive for the students and as a result the sessions are relaxed and enjoyable for both trainers and participants. Staff who use the boards regularly have stated that they would "hate to go back to the old style projection units" (staff feedback form) as the boards allow more movement around the room to highlight important areas of a database and offer more chances to engage the audience.

Feedback from students and academics has been equally positive. On evaluation forms students highlight the interaction of the sessions and several have mentioned the IWB as a specific reason for their enjoyment of the session:
"Very clear and interactive so time flew by!"
"[I enjoyed the] Demo on IWB."

---

[11] For more information on ACTIVstudio and ACTIVote see The Promethean Centre of Excellence at: http://www.ioe.mmu.ac.uk/promethean/

"The demonstration on the IWB was really useful."

"It was great seeing the IWB used to its full potential."

Although tutor feedback is more anecdotal, a number of librarians have received positive comments from academics on the use of the IWB as a training tool. In fact, some library staff have even been asked to provide training for academics in the use of IWBs. Academics have been impressed by the library's use of them and this has heightened their view of the library as a forward thinking service.

The library's investment in IWBs has led to a need to train library staff to ensure that IWBs are used to their full potential. In December 2005, the Training and Development Librarian and the InfoSkills team ran an 'Introduction to Interactive Whiteboards' training day. The aim was to introduce staff to the IWBs, show them a range of the boards' functions and illustrate various ways to use the boards in library training sessions. The day began with training delivered by an instructor from Promethean[12] and was followed by hands-on small group workshops led by InfoSkills team members. These workshops highlighted features of IWBs that are particularly suited to InfoSkills training and involved participants in a variety of games and other whiteboard activities, encouraging them to have fun whilst using the technology in a practical way. The InfoSkills team felt it was crucial that staff enjoyed using the boards and that they gained useful experience within a comfortable environment so that they would be confident when subsequently integrating IWBs into their future teaching.

Due to limited space only key members of staff who deliver training at each site were invited to the session, with the expectation that they would cascade training down to other staff at their local library. To help with this, workshop materials were offered to everyone in attendance so that they could run similar sessions for colleagues. Although InfoSkills team members offered to assist in training at each site, staff were encouraged to lead IWB training at their own libraries so that a sense of ownership of the technology would be developed at the local level. It is hoped that such delegation will lead to greater usage and adoption of the IWBs across all MMU libraries.

Nevertheless, as certain obstacles to library-wide adoption of the IWBs were anticipated, the InfoSkills team developed measures to address these challenges. Some staff members who attended the training day were initially uneasy about the responsibility of training colleagues in the use of technology with which they were still relatively unfamiliar. To help them disseminate information to others and to reinforce their own learning, the InfoSkills team created a 'Guide to ACTIVstudio2 and the Interactive Whiteboards', made available to all staff on the Library Intranet. Although there are comprehensive training guides available from the software supplier, the in-house guides are more accessible and relevant to InfoSkills training. For further training and guidance,

---

[12] MMU's IWBs are supplied by Promethean Ltd. For more information on Promethean go to:
http://www.prometheanworld.com/uk/index.shtml

an INFORMS online guide[13] with step-by-step instructions for using ACTIVstudio software was also created. This is intended for use at the desktop and allows staff to familiarise themselves with the software prior to delivering an InfoSkills session. Finally, a WIKI was set up on the Intranet providing an opportunity for staff to discuss experiences or difficulties and to share ideas across all library sites. It is also used to advertise future sessions using IWBs so staff can observe colleagues using them in a practical way.

Even after receiving training and practicing using the boards, a minority of staff were still not confident about using them in actual teaching sessions. The InfoSkills team acknowledged that for this reason adoption could be slow and encouraged staff to integrate IWBs into their classes incrementally at their own speed. A checklist of four competency levels was created covering basic functions, PowerPoint tools, Flipcharts, and advanced functions, each with a set of specific goals for incorporating IWBs into training sessions. These goals provide trainers with clear tasks to undertake in their sessions, which increase in difficulty and help build confidence as each new level is reached. By monitoring staff progress through their checklists, the InfoSkills team also has the opportunity to measure the ways in which IWBs have been used in the classroom and the degree to which they have been adopted. This information will be used to produce statistics about IWB usage but all names will remain confidential.

It was anticipated that there would be a greater degree of unwillingness amongst staff to use IWBs than there has been. In fact, the IWBs seem to have encouraged staff to become more interactive in their training sessions. Where staff previously may have been reluctant to go beyond the safety of standard PowerPoint presentations and demonstrations, IWBs have become a vehicle for getting staff interested in experimenting in the classroom and engaging more with the audience. To this end, IWBs have actually helped build confidence in teaching.

Since reluctance to integrate the IWB in InfoSkills sessions has not occurred, progression with this new technology has been quicker than expected. Feedback from library sites has been positive and staff are becoming so comfortable with the boards that there now appears to be an unwillingness to teach without them. The InfoSkills team now needs to look to the future to ensure that the level of enthusiasm is maintained and that all new members of library staff are fully trained and continue to incorporate the IWB and its software into their sessions. As ownership of the technology is taken on by library staff, each site will be able to use the technology to suit their purposes and their environments. However, the InfoSkills team will need to continually be aware of how IWBs are being used across sites in order to gather examples of good practice. This will feed back into the development and enhancement of future materials. This will feed back

---

[13] To view the online guide go to: http://inhale.hud.ac.uk/perl/jump.pl?28-2255

into the development and enhancement of future materials and the team envisage that IWBs will become an integral part of MMU's InfoSkills teaching.

References

Becta (2004). ICT in schools survey 2004 [online]. London: DfES [accessed 21 March 2006]. Available at:
  http://www.becta.org.uk/page_documents/research/ict_in_schools_survey_2004.pdf
Philipp, S., and Schmidt, H. (2004). Optimizing learning and retention through interactive lecturing: using the
  Audience Response System (ARS) at CUMC [online]. Center for Education Research and Evaluation:
  Columbia University [accessed 28 January 2006]. Available at:
  http://library.cpmc.columbia.edu/core/web/facultydev/ARS_handout_2004_overview.pdf
Promethean Ltd. (2004). Interactive Whiteboards. new tools, new pedagogies, new learning [online].
  [accessed 2 February 2006]. Available at: http://virtuallearning.org.uk/iwb/Views_from_practitioners.pdf
TechLearn (no date). Interactive whiteboards in education [online]. York: Joint Information Systems
  Committee [accessed 2 February 2006]. Available at:
  http://www.jisc.ac.uk/uploaded_documents/Interactivewhiteboards.pdf

Keeping up with the Google generation: the challenge for Information Literacy teachers

Peter Godwin - London South Bank University

Abstract

Students continue to seek quick answers and instant gratification in their information searching. Google and other search engines are a natural solution. Now Google Scholar aids the possible demise of systematic searching of specific "library" databases. Federated searching via metasearch engines as a library solution often appears cumbersome and unsatisfactory. Librarians need to embrace all the new searching methods, assisting the development of Google Scholar and promoting it alongside subject databases and federated searching at the appropriate level. This paper concludes with the challenges posed to the way librarians teach information literacy today.

Introduction

Librarians are worried. Students, especially in their first year, think they know how to use the Web. Google seems to have endless ambitious all-embracing projects (e.g. Google Print, Google Maps) and Google Scholar promises to filter to scholarly material, thereby threatening librarians in their own territory. Federated searching also implies dumbing down of search abilities. The response in the profession is mixed. Some decline to teach Google Scholar, and some decry metasearch for the harm in can do in fostering "good enough" results.(Frost, 2004) This challenges the clear preference by many patrons for quick and dirty searching. This has profound effects on the way we teach information literacy. We shall consider the situation outlined above and then concentrate on how it impacts on our teaching.

The Net Generation students

Let us begin with our users. Increasingly they have grown up with PCs and video games, working in groups, multitasking and working things out for themselves without the use of manuals. (Lippincott, 2005). This Net Generation expects a single search box like Google or Amazon to give instant satisfaction. They say "I'll Google it" and they guess that their present research needs and what they need to know for the rest of their lives can be answered by a Google search. The LibQUAL survey in 2003 across ARL libraries showed that twice as many users accessed library resources via a web page daily as use the resources on the premises and of these same users over 4 times as many use Yahoo, Google or other non-library gateways daily. Library databases are too difficult to access, and are often not situated in the environment where the student works, i.e. a VLE. They are not inclined to come to our IL sessions because they do not perceive the need and do not get enthusiastic about Boolean or controlled vocabulary searching. As Roy Tennant has said "Only librarians enjoy looking for information. Everyone else just wants to be able to use the information and would really prefer that it was just handed to them." (Tennant, 2001) We disregard exactly how today's students want to operate. They do not want training which makes them into librarians and they do not want to ask a librarian how to retrieve information! This was the conclusion of Kate Wittenberg's 3 year study of research habits across the United Sates.(Hafner, 2004). In the UK in the EDNER Project showed students prefer to locate information via a search engine above other options and that Google is the main choice.(Griffiths and Brophy, 2003 and 2006). Also that they are content with "good enough for the purpose", certainly at lower levels of research.

Google and Google Scholar

Google is currently the first choice search engine for most tutors and students. The Google empire is now enormous and includes: Google Print Publisher Program to include all text of public domain books and a few sample pages from books still in print. Google Print Library Project to digitise the content of a number of large research libraries in the US and UK. A host of other Google services, most notably Google Scholar (GS) launched to "allow and enable users to search for scholarly literature located across the Web" (Anurag Acharya, Google Scholar) Other similar products from Yahoo and Microsoft are under development. Google Scholar is a slice of Google from the open web which is scholarly, plus as much publishers' material as Google is allowed to crawl over, display and index. GS has harvested metadata from various journal publishers so that users can access content from one interface. GS links to material in institutional repositories and new digitisation initiatives like the Google Print at the Bodleian and the JISC Information Environment. It links to ingenta and hence to an institution's full text holdings. GS also links to the OCLC WorldCat thereby giving library locations for individual items. Much has been written about the deficiencies of GS (Myhill, 2005). However, it is only a beta product. Used with some caution alongside Google it can provide useful quick results for student research in science and technology. Its main shortfalls are that its coverage in humanities and social science is weak and in all subjects it gives many abstracts which then do not link to full text without payment. This is being overcome as libraries are seeking ways of linking to their full text journals. For example, Michigan State University and Oregon State University are working on a project whereby Millennium, Innovative's library management system, automatically creates the institutional journal holdings data to inform GS. (Innovative Interfaces, 2005). Then their library users can link via WebBridge, a smart-linking tool, to connect to the full text of their journals. For example, University of California, San Francisco have listed Google Scholar with their databases, and are being proactive in their teaching about it and have linked to the full text of their journals.

Metasearch

A realisation that we will need to adapt our systems rather than our users has led to the use of meta search facilities offered by the library management system providers which can search across library catalogues, databases and the web or a combination of these. This avoids the need to search several databases and learning their different characteristics, and appears to give ready results. As with GS, best results come from distinct subjects from the sciences rather than indistinct searches from the "softer" subjects. These commercial metasearch engines may jumble too much together, giving good enough rather than truly comprehensive research results. With incompatible databases linked together there is limited ability to perform complex searches.

How does this affect Information Literacy?

We cannot change our users' preference for using Google or GS. Nor should we fail to recommend it or metasearch engines for certain types of information searching. "As service providers and developers, it is crucial that we learn lessons from those commercial search engines that dominate students' use and embed those lessons into academic resources that students can find and use easily" (Griffiths and Brophy, 2006).But how does this affect Information Literacy? Before we look at how this analysis affects our teaching we must be clear about what we mean by Information Literacy (IL). Librarians continue to agonise over definitions. There should be a basic level of agreement across the profession based on the Council of Australian University Librarians definition, 2001, ACRL division of the American Library Association, 2000, the UNESCO meeting of Information Literacy experts in Prague, 2003, the Seven Pillars model developed by SCONUL, in the UK, and the recent CILIP definition in the UK applicable to all communities. I sympathise with Edward Owushu-Ansah (2003) who forcibly makes the point that we have to move on from the obsession with definitions. The confusion equating information literacy with IT literacy still continues. Certainly basic IT skills underpin information skills and the two skill sets intertwine throughout their different levels. However, the assumption by academics that IT skills (using a computer and searching the internet) somehow equip the student to be a competent information searcher still requires correction. For simplicity I shall use the SCONUL Seven Pillars model as the point of reference for how the changes in technology and searching behaviour can affect our teaching.

Effects on teaching of Information Literacy

The Net Generation will no longer want to be taught about libraries from an organisational context. According to Lippincott (2005) we should consider linking through course management systems (VLEs) using tutorials, exercises, games and even simulations. Blogs could be started by libraries and used by students exchanging valuable information resources. Yi (2005) also sees the future in terms of IL online, linked to faculty course pages. Electronic delivery of IL has already been seen as an alternative to class teaching but today's students may be more interested and engaged in these online methods. This could imply that we become more " the guide on the side" advising by e-mail, and via VLEs with less emphasis on class teaching and enquiry desks. Turning to how the skills in the SCONUL model may be affected :

Skill 1 Recognising an information need : the proliferation of information sources makes the problem of information overload even greater. The digitisation of special collections, e.g. news archives and library collections, means that the student is overwhelmed by the quantity of available material. The ease of Google and GS and metasearch tools' ability to cross search these resources makes the need to be able to define the topic and know the context of their research critical. Society is becoming "information-rich but question-poor" according to Baroness Greenfield. (Cochrane, 2003) We help them to formulate questions as well and give answers. (Willis, 2005). Alan Bundy said "Sheer abundance of information and technology will not in itself create more informed citizens without a complementary understanding and capacity to use information effectively"(Bundy, 2004).

Skill 2 Distinguishing sources and access : the use of GS and meta search will increase amounts of material easily traceable. The chunks of information can seem decontextualised and their origins appear blurred. This will continue as books become available for purchase by chapter. Now librarians are encouraging students to consider whether they should be considering a book, professional or academic journal, encyclopedia etc. to fill their information need. Cross search reduces this requirement. The need to distinguish document types diminishes and no longer will it be important to point users to particular information carriers or parts of a building (Campbell 2004). They are making their preference for electronic easy access where they are quite clear. Users will pay less attention to the category of the information carrier or container and more to the reliability of the information.(Skill 5)

Skill 3 Constructing search strategies : merging of catalogues and databases and web sites means that searching can be easier at lower levels. This stems from the ability to cross search databases across subjects and catalogues overcoming different interfaces and authentication problems. How to use keywords has always been a major problem for students. Google and the metasearch engines have made this easier, and the user gets some kind of response. However, the need to understand how to input the right keywords and adjust these remains a key skill. As Rochelle Mazar (2005) said "Searching the internet is like drawing; you sketch out the general shape first, look at it, consider it, and start filling in details here and there". Interestingly, Brophy and Bawden (2005) in their comparison of search results from Google and library resources found that improving the skills of users is likely to give better results from library systems, but not from Google. At present, librarians still have a role in helping users select the appropriate search tool and pointing out the deficiencies. The need to teach which search tool is most appropriate becomes less important with metasearching, and the blurring of boundaries. E.g. SCOPUS includes Web sites with its search. We can always expect users to prefer the easier, faster solutions, giving good enough results, rather than seeking comprehensiveness.

Skill 4 Locating and accessing: access is increasingly through one box, with little need to learn complex search interfaces. Therefore less time need be spent on this skill. However the importance of good keyword search technique at all levels remains. The quality of the metasearch product and the ability of the library to customise it are important in how best to consider using it in teaching. Some libraries with metasearch (McCaskie, 2004) indicated that there is less need to spend time at lower levels on particular databases and spend more time on generic skills, perhaps using a metasearch engine, so that they can use any database. (McCaskie, 2004). We have to decide how best to recommend the use of these search tools. At lower levels GS and Google will give provide a good starting point and could be used developing keyword search skills. There is debate about how metasearch is best used. Higher level searching can be assisted by a basic search on a metasearch engine, which provides guidance of which databases to follow up with specific searches accomplished using search terms geared to that particular database. Here the librarian must assist the user who is accustomed to lazy searching via Google, GS or a metasearch engine.

Skill 5 Comparing and evaluating : all the trends so far mentioned require development of skills to critically evaluate the amassed material. Students have always been poor evaluators, and the results of quick and easy searches through Google accentuate this. A recent article by James Hooks (2005) on IL for off-campus stresses importance of critical thinking skills. With metasearch the importance of evaluation is also stressed. (McCaskie, 2004). Bundy (2004) emphasises "critical discernment and reasoning" as the most important element of IL. Critical thinking and the ability to compare and evaluate are the skills which should be concentrated upon now. (Wallis, 2005)(Campbell (2004) (Terrell 2004). This is unfortunate because it is often a skill that librarians feel least comfortable about, and regard as the province of academics or study skills advisers. Many IL sites spend far more time on searching rather than evaluating information. Yet this is the area for development that arises from the foregoing. It is likely to be much more difficult to assess the value and validity of the mass of information sources culled from GS or a metasearch than from a single database. Visual clues may be less prominent in the records. In fact Google and GS is renowned for giving relevant results and the meta search engines work differently and may simply rank by date and the separate databases and sources.

Skill 6 Organising, applying and communicating: This group of skills can also be expected to become more important in IL teaching. This can lead to increased respect for the role of librarians (Boden and Carroll, 2006).The blurring of where information comes from could impair the ability of users to understand ethical, legal and social issues regarding the use of information. Plagiarism will be more tempting, and this area demands librarian involvement. This will need to include the cultural variations in what is acceptable in the use of information. (Campbell 2004). Jude Carroll noted in Crace (2005) that with search engines this became more of a problem in the United States in 1998 at these became live. Tutors do not realise that many students find information searching uninteresting and will simply copy and paste. Referencing (especially electronic) will become a more important skill. In the past this has suffered through lack of time. Bibliographic software output may improve and make referencing easier. The different databases on a metasearch may make this difficult but the aspiration is worth considering.

Skill 7 Synthesising and adding new knowledge: This skill really only applies to higher levels of IL and as Terrell (2004) says, is not affected provided they have got the right information and have evaluated it correctly!

Conclusion

All these changes imply the need for more cooperation with academic staff. If online courses are to become important then they must be developed with tutors' participation. Plagiarism is a major academic consideration and our interest is likely to be welcomed by them, thus helping us to develop into other IL areas. Staff realise they need librarians in the fight against Googlisation (Yi, 2005). I believe we should recommend the whole portfolio of tools including Google, GS, gateways, or our own databases according to the level and subject area. Evaluation of web sites and information in general should become central to our programmes. Richard Sweeney, encapsulated it in Kenney (2004) by saying " The most effective way to draw users to high-quality research is both to help users to formulate Google searches and to think critically. That's our future". In order for this to work we must have the confidence to teach this with the support of the academic staff. Hence, the emphasis and time spent by librarians within the skills should be adjusted according to the technological changes and need to communicate with the Net Generation of students. If we work to adapt our library systems rather than our users, we have an excellent chance of meeting their needs. Ultimately we must seek to be where we they are, mediating, advising, entertaining, leading them toward the elusive goal of Information Literacy.

References

Boden, D and Carroll, J (2006) Combatting plagiarism through information literacy. Library and Information Update. 5, (1-2) : 40-41.

Brophy, J. and Bawden, D.(2005) Is Google enough? Comparison of an internet search engine with academic library resources. Aslib Proceedings : New Information Perspectives 57 (6) : 498-512

Bundy, A.(2004) One essential direction : information literacy, information technology fluency. Journal of eLiteracy, 1: 7-22.

Campbell, S.(2004) Defining Information Literacy in the 21st Century. World Library and Information Congress : 70th IFLA General Conference and Council, 22-27 August 2004 Buenos Aires, available at www.ifla.org/IV/ifla70/papers/059e-Campbell.pdf   (accessed 2 March 2006).

Carlson, S. (2003) New allies in the fight against research by Googling. Chronicle of Higher Education, 49 (28) : A33.

Cochrane, N. (2003) Too much information. The Age 11 Nov .available at http://www.theage.com.au/cgi-bin/common/popupPrintArticle.pl?path=/articles/2003/11/10/1068329472603.html

Crace, J.(2005) Original thinker : Jude Carroll, leading authority on plagiarism, talks to John Crace about ethics and the Google generation. Guardian 26 April : 20.

Frost, W.J.(2004) Do we want or need metasearching? Library Journal 129 (6): 68.

Griffiths, J.R.and Brophy, P.(2006)   Student searching behavior and the web : use of academic resources and Google. Library Trends 53 (4) : 539-554.

Griffiths, J.R.and Brophy, P. (2003) Student searching behaviour in the JISC Information Environment. Ariadne. 33.

Hafner, K. (2004) Old search engine, the library, tries to fit into a Google world. New York Times 21 June.

Hooks, J.D. and Corbett, F.jr. (2005) Information literacy for off-campus graduate cohorts. Library Review 54 (4) : 245-256.

Innovative Interfaces. (2005) Innovative libraries extend into Google Scholar. Inn-Touch 19 :2 : 2

Kenney, B. (2004) Googlizers vs. resistors. Library Journal 129 (20) :44-46

Lippincott, J.K.(2005) Net generation students and libraries. In Educating the Net Generation, edited by D.G. and J.L Oblinger. Educause at http://www.educause.edu/educatingthenetgen accessed 2 March 2006.

Mazar, R.A.(2005) Search strings and information literacy. Random Access Mazar at http://www.mazar.ca/2005/02/22/search-strings-and-information-literacy/ accessed 26 Feb 2006

McCaskie, L.(2004)What are the implications for Information Literacy training in Higher Education with the introduction of federated search engines? Study for Master of Arts in Librarianship at University of Sheffield, Sept. 2004 available at http://dagda.shef.ac.uk/dissertations/2003-04/External/McCaskie_Lucy_MALib.pdf   acc 2 March 2006.

Myhill, M.(2005) Just what I wanted! The perfect Christmas gift – Google Scholar – or is it? SCONUL Focus 34 Spring : 42-44

Owusu-Ansah, E.K. (2003)Information literacy and the academic library : a critical look at a concept and the controversies surrounding it. Journal of Academic Librarianship 29 (4) : 219-230

Tennant, R. (2001) Digital Libraries – cross-database search : one-stop shopping. Library Journal 126 (17) : 29.

Terrell, J. (2004) Cross-database Searching: Information Literacy for the Real World? [online]. In: Managing Information in the Digital Age: The Australian Technology Network Libraries Respond; pages: 117-132. Huthwaite, Ann (Editor). Adelaide: University of South Australia Library for the Librarians of the Australian Technology Network, 2005. Available at http://search.informit.com.au/documentSummary;dn=934504500450143;res=E-LIBRARY. accessed1 March 2006.

Willis (2005) Cyberspace, information literacy and the information society. Library Review 54 (2) : 218-222.

Yi, H. (2005) Library instruction goes online. Library Review 54 (1) : 47

Information overload and the re-invention of brutality: a systemic view of information literacy

Tony Brauer - Library and Information Service, Buckinghamshire Chilterns University College

Abstract: From a systemic perspective, our descriptions of the world reflect uncertainty, complexity, and interconnectedness. In order to understand and interact with our worlds, we need a depth and breadth of understanding that is not adequately served by the search engine, which depends inherently on the reduction of the complex to series of discrete terms. A consequence of this may be to reinforce respect for superficial knowledge at the expense of understanding, a form of brutality, simply because the technology is convenient.

Thirty years ago, in Trafalgar Square, I came across four young people looking at a street map. They were wondering where to go. I suggested the National Gallery.

One of them replied,
"I did Art Appreciation at West Texas U, so I guess I've already seen all that."

Fair enough; but is there not a difference between the image projected on to a screen, and the original? Does that difference not tell us anything about the relations between data, information, knowledge, and wisdom? Furthermore, could it be that search engines privileges facts over ideas?

Intuitively, one might say not. The world-wide-web is thronged with statements of opinion. Indeed, one of the recognised difficulties of the web is that it is indiscriminate; but from this stems the recognition that opinion on the net is not information. It is crude data. Having seen an image or heard a sound, one knows only that someone somewhere purports to see merit in a certain arrangement of symbols.

If the symbols are to achieve meaning, they require evaluation; and perhaps evaluation is a process through which data is transformed into information by being placed in context. If so, the continuing broadening of context may enrich information so that it becomes knowledge, and, by extension, wisdom.

Linguistic philosophy could support that view. The grand projects of the logical positivists sought to demonstrate that meaning inhered specifically to individual symbols, which could then become the building blocks of rigorously impregnable edifices: and, of course, the projects failed. Russell and Whitehead in mathematics and formal logic, and Wittgenstein in language found themselves denying that which they had sought to demonstrate. Language, in its many forms, is more like Ryle's games, or Quine's ephemeral webs of meaning.

This is consistent with the suggestion that data becomes information through contextualisation; and, if this is the case, search engines may be the catalyst of the re-invention of brutality. Such sweeping statements may not reflect the balance that is associated with wisdom, so that it seems appropriate to explore a little further how this general proposition might apply to academic endeavour, both theoretical and practical.

Human welfare offers a rich field of exploration, conjoining, as it does, highly abstract scientific exploration with practical ends, with each aspect bathed in metaphysical speculation about the value of individual lives and of life itself.

In the practical realm, O'Sullivan's (2005) thoughts on the nature of practice wisdom are helpful. He contrasts the more reductive perspective on social work that is rooted in competences, protocols, and evidence-based practice, with the acceptance of tacit knowledge, experience, intuitive judgements, and the integration of the philosophies of the worker and the client (O'Sullivan, 2005:222).

Of course there are those who would then characterise wisdom, in this latter sense, as unreliable and idiosyncratic (ibid). However, placed in the context of reflective judgement, the picture may alter. Following, Kitchener and Brenner (1990), O'Sullivan represents reflective judgement in terms of four characteristics: inherent complexity, uncertainty, the need for breadth and depth of comprehension, and the capacity to respond effectively.

There are ways in which a search engine could contribute in such circumstances, but probably only by redirecting the actor towards other sources. Reflective judgement is dependent on the capacity to formulate appropriate questions from a wide range of often conflicting data. It requires integration. The mode of selection of a search engine is quite simply reductive. It relies on matching term with term in the most literal reductive way. This assertion may be simply evaluated by entering the search term wisdom into a search engine such as Google.

The argument thus far suggests the following: that if the purpose of enquiry is to contribute effectively and beneficially to human welfare, search engines may be inherently inadequate; and, by creating an illusion of adequacy, may distract from the more complex processes necessary to achieve the purpose as described.

A counter-argument might, however, be presented: that this argument only applies at the level of practical intervention, and that at more abstract levels there is a clear and unmitigated truth; or at least a convergence that can readily be identified by searching the web.

The field of human welfare again offers opportunities for exploring the theme, this time in its epistemological dimension.

Over the last 20 years, the theory of evidence-based medical intervention has become the dominant ideology in medicine in Britain, at least. The problem has been expressed concisely, if perhaps rather opaquely, by Clark (1998:1246):

The contextually bound nature of research findings, consequential in the acknowledgement of researcher and theoretical biases, warrants that knowledge deemed to be 'truthful' under post-positivistic inquiry is not universally generalizable to all cases and all situations.

An illustration may help. Evidence based medicine suggests that since, let us say, recurrence of heart failure in middle aged men Is reduced by x% (where x > 50) through the use of a cocktail of pharmaceuticals, it is the appropriate treatment for middle aged men who have had serious heart attacks.

What if the origins of the heart attack lie not in the physical domain on which the pharmaceuticals act, but in the psychological, social, or (as some would argue) the spiritual realm? Where the origins of the problem lie is probably where the problem must be addressed.

What has occurred is that the scientific paradigm has been privileged, not because science provides irrefutable truths, but, quite possibly, simply because it offers an excellent defence against accusations of irresponsibility; and that may be because it is simple and clear cut. All complexities and uncertainties are cast aside by *ceteris paribus* – "other things being equal" – which, of course, they never are.

The classic metaphor for this approach is the story of the drunk on a cold dark night, staggering about under the lamp-post. The beat copper – this is an old story – approaches him and asks him what he is doing.

"I'm looking for my keys"
"You lost them here, then?"
"No, but it's the easiest place to look."

The point of this story is probably self-evident. For all the efforts by scientists, creationists, and other grand narrators to assert a single all encompassing truth, it remains elusive. We live, even in the most abstract fields, amid paradox, uncertainty, and complexity.

It is at this point that the theory of language reasserts its presence. Language does not attach itself unambiguously to the universe. Consider simply that when the term *freedom* is translated between American and Japanese its connotations may change from the unassailable right to individual choice to freedom from the fear of acting contrary to social mores.

If one seeks to overturn this problem by an appeal to the more rigorous languages of mathematics or formal logic, consider the square root of minus one, or Russell's paradox (i.e. Whether the set of all sets which are not members of themselves is a member of itself or not?). Language offers neither inherent certainty, nor ostensive precision.

Whether the world is essentially simple, and it is merely our attempts to describe it that are complex and confused, is a moot point. Search engines, however, work immutably in the realm of language and symbols; and in that medium, the world is complex, uncertain, ambiguous, and paradoxical.

This is not to argue that language cannot inform our understanding and mediate our interactions. Rather, it is to claim that it is at best naïve to rely on reductive language to provide an accurate, abstract replication of any set of phenomena.

Yet what more can a search engine do?

From the examples given above it can be inferred that at all levels of enquiry we need to take account of the systemic characteristics of interconnectedness, uncertainty, complexity, in which the characteristics of the whole cannot be predicted by the summation of the components. The limitations of language have been attested. How then could we possibly hope to achieve anything approaching practical or esoteric wisdom by relying on a mechanism that simply attaches to one or a few components, and seeks to find other instances of their contiguous occurrence, irrespective of their context?

A search engine cannot surface the tacit, or nurture an emergent. It can only see where a set of symbols has been used elsewhere.

This it does well. I freely admit that I located the examples for practice and theory that I have used – O'Sullivan and Clark - through the use of a search engine. If I feel no shame, it is because, while I identified a possible set through the search engine, the selection and interpretation of the examples was dependent on experience and training; on the capacity to evaluate a document against the theoretical background derived from scholarship, and the practical experience of previous conferences.

It is these skills that enable me to cope with uncertainty, complexity, and context-dependence. These are the keys to understanding our experiences, and thence to our capacity to react constructively.

However, when in academic libraries we see the abandonment of books in favour of the screen and keyboard, we are witnessing a revolution in search patterns. The selection of specific search terms encourages the capture of narrow and specific data. That which we capture through the selection of a book, if we select wisely, is data set into an interpretive context. We need not lose our critical faculties in reading, but, by having the data set in relation to other data, our evaluative capacity for each set of data is immeasurably increased.

Long live books. Long may art and intuition be valued. Long may I be able to sit and learn in the National Gallery, as I did recently, for an hour or so, in the company of Canaletto and a view of the Grand Canal. I can't be certain how my familiarity with Shakespeare, Heller, Chevalier, Chesterton, Venice, Budapest and Cluj informed my understanding. Nevertheless, although uncertain as to the process, I sincerely believe that there is a critically significant difference between the contextualised understanding of the painting, and that which can be achieved by seeing the image projected onto a screen at the University of West Texas.

Internet searching and the reinvention of brutality, then: a future in which people can, for a remarkably low price, locate the facts about anything; but who will uncover the value of nothing. Big on quantity, for certain, but, it would appear, regrettably low on quality.

References

Clark, A.M., (1998) The qualitative-quantitative debate: moving from positivism and confrontation to post-positivism and reconciliation, Journal of Advanced Nursing 27:1242-1249

Kitchener, K.S. and Brenner, H.G. (1990) 'Wisdom and Reflective Judgement: Knowing in the Face of Uncertainty', in R. J. Sternberg (ed). Wisdom: Its Nature, Origins and Development, pp. 212–27. Cambridge: Cambridge University Press.

O'Sullivan, I (2005) Some theoretical propositions on the nature of practical wisdom, Journal of Social Work 5(2):221-242

Working towards the Information Literate University

Sheila Webber - Senior Lecturer, Department of Information Studies, University of Sheffield
Bill Johnston - Senior Lecturer, Centre for Academic Practice and Learning Enhancement, University of Strathclyde

Introduction

Universities are challenged in many ways: measured, questioned, and criticised. In this paper we develop the concept of the Information Literate University (ILU), and propose that by moving towards the goal of becoming an ILU, universities could meet some of these challenges. We draw on visions of the ILU provided by academics in four disciplines, contributed as part of a research project. We also identify some characteristics of library progress towards the ILU. Our own definition of information literacy is "the adoption of appropriate information behaviour to obtain, through whatever channel or medium, information well fitted to information needs, together with critical awareness of the importance of wise and ethical use of information in society." (Johnston and Webber, 2004, 3)

What do we mean by the Information Literate University?

We started developing our idea of the ILU several years ago. It emerged from our concept of the 'information literate person in the changing world', identifying factors in the internal and external world that may require a person to develop his/her information literacy through the course of his/her life. Examples of these factors are: changing personal goals and priorities; the changing legal and ethical framework; and the information culture of the organisation that person works in.

However, personal information literacy is not enough. Indeed personal information literacy cannot be developed fully without support from the external environment, including the environment in which one studies and works. We were stimulated by our understanding of the learning organisation; defined as one which "facilitates the learning of all its members and continually transforms itself" (Pedler et al., 1989: 2) Additionally, UK Higher Education is being challenged to find new organisational and curricula forms which are not based on disciplinary "silos" (Macfarlane and Ottewill, 2001).

If organisations are truly to "learn" then they need employees who are able to identify when they need to learn, who can find out what the opportunities are for learning, and are able to find, use and communicate information as an integral part of their learning. The organisation itself needs to have procedures, policies, rewards, networks and services in place that encourage and enable organisational as well as individual learning to take place. This means people learning from each other, but also people empowered to change how the organisation works and even its goals and outcomes, in the light of new knowledge. We have developed a diagram of the ILU (unfortunately, it is not possible to reproduce this here). The diagram identifies as linked constituents of the ILU:

- Management for information literacy: strategy, resourcing, policy and infrastructure;
- Information literate research;
- Information literate students and graduates;
- Information literate curriculum; acknowledging information literacy as a subject of study, and encompassing learning, teaching and assessment;
- Staff development for information literacy;
- Information literate librarians.

Our vision of the ILU requires everyone in the university become information literate, whether administrators, students, researchers, librarians or academics. Management for information literacy implies rethinking internal communication and structures. It could also mean greater ability to function as a knowledge-creating organisation and more a creative response to an increasingly complex external environment. *Academic peers elsewhere* and the *Wider society* (including employers) are also represented on our diagram as elements in the ILU. An ILU can be seen as a response to a fast changing Information Society.

The main way in which we have been collecting other academics' views about the ILU is through our project on UK academics' conceptions of information literacy (Webber et al, 2005; Webber and Johnston 2005), funded by the Arts and Humanities Research Council. The last question which Stuart Boon, our research associate, asked in the interviews was 'What is your conception of the Information Literate University?'. Of the 80 academics he interviewed (in Marketing, English, Civil Engineering and Chemistry) only a couple baulked at the question. Most interviewees took the opportunity to think beyond their current constraints, to sketch out a utopia (or occasionally, a dystopia) and think about what was needed to achieve change.

Academics and the ILU

Some key themes emerged: more interaction and sharing within and beyond the university, more access, better IT, better learning and teaching. We will illustrate some of those ideas here: interviewees are represented by the name of their discipline and a number between 1 and 20 allocated within each discipline.

There were a few cases where the response seemed to arise from fundamental beliefs about what a university stood for: "It would be unacceptable not to be a university that is information literate' (Chemistry 16) For a few academics this meant that it was a "paradox" to suggest that a university was not an ILU: "Any university, even if it's crap—they have to impart information, they have to be a reservoir of information. There have to be levels of information literacy present. That much is transparent. Otherwise we could not call ourselves universities." (Marketing 04). However, at the other end of the scale, a number of academics felt that not only was their university not information literate, but that it would take a good deal to make it so (according to one academic it would need "a bomb"!)

A variety of possible goals for the ILU emerged. One focus was the student learning experience, for example: 'Just more learning. It's as simple as better, fuller, student learning experience that goes beyond the confines of the classroom and the university, and you know, better research, more informed research.' (English 16) This could reach beyond the university 'to teach students better: to give them, not just more information, but more skills and more confidence they can go out and they can have a good life with.' (English 07)

As an extension of this, all staff are seen as skilled and benefiting from their information literacy in an ILU "A university where everyone, professors, students, professional staff, are all literate with information. I suppose where everyone involved is comfortable with information and its use. Everyone knows how to access it and retrieve it. Everyone knows how to use it for their benefit, possibly for everyone's benefit. " (Marketing 09)

This flags up a focus on increased access and sources, and the skills to exploit this, which was the central idea for some: 'the aim would be to make available every bit of information that is possible to have accessible' (Chemistry 16); 'to be able to use information more efficiently and accurately, of course' (Engineering 18). "I think it was a sort of kind of utopia where people knew [laughs] about internal information and links to external information that would avoid wasting time ..." (Civil Engineering 10) To achieve this version of the ILU you need 'big enough computer labs' (English 01), 'access to a lot of quality databases' (Chemistry 08) and 'the best software packages.' (Chemistry 16) However there is the danger of information overload, so filters are needed too: "It would be nice to have a personal [librarian], wouldn't it? [snickers] Somebody who would literally sit outside your office and stop all this information coming in unless you wanted it, that would be literally speaking, but they could be anywhere in the library I suppose. " (Marketing 18)

The focus was not just on technology and traditional information. For some, the goal would be interaction, communication and knowledge creation. "Flexible access that, um, and access that creates a much more of a synergistic interaction between the academics and the librarians." (Chemistry 18) 'I don't know that I would be doing anything differently..., it would just be that I would have so much more freedom to interact and engage with others.' (English 13)

Some of the visions that we found most exciting talked about development and creativity. An ILU might have a more meaningful and creative relationship with the information society around it – including the local society:

'I might be expecting to work, well, be more involved in the local community, being more obviously tied to a city and a place, and, know more about what is going on, a more holistic view of the university's place, and what's happening across the university. I might be able to deploy all the resources of the library rather than just the ones I have encountered so far, and I would be able to do that in a way that is both meaningful to me, to my students, and also to those from outside who might be peers.' (English 08)
'it's almost like an ideal like an exchange of knowledge and experience and skills, um… and an university that is highly information literate would provide access to information and advice to a much larger constituency than just students [   ] an information literate university, I would say, Is one that enables those kinds of enriching process of where people interact in many, many unplanned and unlooked-for ways, but you have to enable that… you need buildings and communication methods that break down barriers and help people to bump into one another so that ideas flow." (Civil Engineering 16)
Thus, communication does not just rely on a good technological infrastructure, it also implies changes in the physical environment and changes in organizational culture.

One lecturer (Marketing 18) expressed the value to the academic, to the university and to others in having this increased access and interchange of ideas:
"all the different departments would be aware of what is going on in departments and in universities[…] so everybody would be in a sort of loop and would know what is going on, because they would have access to all this information that was around—relevant information, so you would be, I suppose, more up to date, more on the ball, more able to do contemporary research, I guess, because you would know what other people are doing, teaching style, teaching content, you would know what other universities are doing for business studies, for example. So you would have more of an idea, rather than sitting in your little—I am not going to say ivory tower, because that is such an old-fashioned phrase—sitting in your office in your university and being isolated, you'd be in contact with relevant people elsewhere, knowing what they are doing, they would know what you are doing, so it would be the dissemination of knowledge as well. It would be easier and more efficient, so that would be a good objective for the university, because that would help with its image, its PR, its standing, especially overseas as well. People would know what you are doing overseas as well, um, so it would be a way of marketing yourself without actually marketing yourself, um… So I think it would be a good objective to go for, a good goal to go for, an information literate university."
This external role is expressed neatly by another lecturer "an ILU would be one that could communicate with the surrounding society about what it's doing and convince or be convincing about its goals or aims" (English 08)

We asked interviewees what they saw as challenges for the ILU. Some people saw their current resources as inadequate (wanting better "kit", improved networking and more journals). Lack of money was identified by some as a barrier, as was lack of time (e.g. lack of time to become educated for the ILU, or to filter out the good information), though for some the ILU would be time *saving*. However, for others, change in attitude or skill level was key to achieving an ILU. Various stakeholders were identified as needing an attitude change: managers, those in Estates, students, and also academics themselves: 'I think all the technological side is there. The challenge would be changing the way that academics provide teaching or learning provision, or whatever you want to call it." (Civil Engineering 19)

The visions of an ILU that emerged from our academics were, as with their conceptions of information literacy itself, diverse. They illuminate and extend parts of our own vision of an ILU. In particular, it was after engaging with the data from our research that we realised the importance of the ILU communicating and interacting with the outside community, and of enabling good communication at all levels within the university.

Librarians and the ILU

A number of documents have been produced by librarians identifying ways in which librarians can put information literacy higher up the agenda, or can measure achievement in progressing information literacy institutionally. Examples are the ACRL "Best practice" guidelines (ACRL, 2002) and the Critical Success Factors (CSFs) developed via workshops organised by the Society for College, National and University Libraries (SCONUL) (Town, 2003). Indicators often include: extent and nature of collaboration with academics; the extent to which information literacy is "embedded" in subjects; mention of information literacy in key documents (e.g. Learning and Teaching Strategy); development of an institutional information literacy framework; library representation on key committees. The SCONUL CSFs identify measures relating to staff, resources, students, partners, strategy and pedagogy.

Our own contribution in this area is a list of characteristics (see Appendix 1) relating to three levels of information literacy: embryonic; intermediate and what we term "Threshold ILU" (note that the "ILU" was not a term actually used in the interviews). Characteristics are identified in relation to Management; Librarians; Approach to learning and teaching; Students; Academics. The lists were developed by Webber, following a visit to Australia in June 2002 which was part-sponsored by the John Campbell Trust. The work was based primarily on informal interviews about information literacy development and strategy with librarians and library managers in five universities (University of South Australia, Adelaide; Queensland University of Technology; University of Queensland; Griffith University; Central Queensland University).

It should be stressed that these universities do not fall into one single category of IL progression, and they were all chosen because they had already engaged with information literacy for some time and had examples of best practice. However, librarians were able to describe past situations, or in other cases the level of advancement was not even in all areas. The characteristics of being on the threshold of an ILU were variously: cited by librarians as things they were proud to have achieved, or which they admired in another programme and would like to emulate, or which formed

46

part of their own vision of a successful information literacy programme; mentioned on institutional websites or observed by Webber during visits. Some data was drawn from articles written by librarians at the institutions concerned, or from presentations at the Lifelong Learning Conference that was part of the same trip. The emphasis on graduate attributes is something which has been important in Australian universities for some time, but it seems to be increasingly relevant in the UK context.

One interesting aspect to emerge was the extent to which key events could move institutions down the information literacy ladder, not just up it. On the whole, one tends to celebrate the catalysts that have produced positive changes. For example, at Sheffield University, collaborative work by academics from different departments on a successful bid for a Centre for Excellence in Teaching and Learning (the CETL CILASS) resulted in greater understanding of information literacy (one of the key elements in the bid) and greater attention at the institutional level (inclusion of information literacy in the Learning, Teaching and Assessment Strategy, which has had beneficial knock-on effects as Departmental versions are developed). However, Webber also heard on her Australian trip of information literacy going **down** the agenda because a new head of Teaching and Learning thought it was "not measurable" and therefore not suitable as a graduate attribute, or of information literacy going off the agenda because it was "last year's theme". It would be useful to investigate these "down" factors more fully.

Towards the ILU

Although the situation may have moved on in the Australian institutions concerned, the characteristics are still recognisable, and certainly there are still not many libraries that have achieved everything in the "Threshold ILU" list. We feel that it can still be useful as a basis for discussion about directions and progress of the library towards an ILU. However, we also realise now that this is not the whole picture. Our AHRC-sponsored research has made us aware of the way in which academics can envision an ILU which extends outside the university, and into all areas of their academic life: teaching, research, administration and professional work. For some, it can extend further, linking the university into society: and not just the society of potential student "customers". Then there are the students themselves, who might well have their own vision of an ILU.

Additionally, there are groups of people who are present in a more shadowy form in both academic and library perspectives on information literacy: namely administrative staff and managers. They tended to emerge from our academics' accounts as, in the main, barriers to IL: people who are failing to provide resources, creating bureaucracy, or blocking innovation. However they are an integral part of a university, and it could be that understanding and acknowledging their needs in an ILU is one of the keys to achievement. Hou (2004) investigated Sheffield University administrators' conceptions of information literacy. One notable aspect which emerges here, as with other research into workplace information behaviour, is the importance of internal and specialist information, and the importance of personal channels of information. Becoming information literate in this environment requires a different kind of education and support than education for "academic" information literacy. Everyone would benefit, though, from a truly information literate university administration.

Key points that emerge are that an ILU does not depend on library activities, and that changes to achieve an ILU require more than librarians' intervention. If one were to design afresh an organisation that was effective at identifying, locating, organising, using and communicating information between all its stakeholders, then the compartmentalised, hierarchical and often secretive university structure is not necessarily one would come up with. Whilst reorganising university structure and curriculum around the concept of information literacy may seem a bold idea, the nature and purpose of universities are already being questioned: challenged by issues of widening participation, employability, globalisation and financial sustainability.

Whether the emphasis is a pragmatic Government view of producing graduates who are able to engage with the world of work, or Barnett's (1997) vision of "higher education for a critical life" with students and academics willing to be challenged by new perspectives, information literacy can be seen as an important factor. However if the institution itself becomes information literate, with systems that reward information literate behaviour and organisational structures that encourage and enable the sort of access and exchange envisioned by our academic interviewees, then it will be a good thing for higher education itself, and not just for librarians.

References

ACRL. (2002) Characteristics of Programs of Information Literacy that Illustrate Best Practices: A Guideline. Washington: ALA. http://www.ala.org/ala/acrl/acrlstandards/characteristics.htm

Barnett, R. (1997) Higher education: a critical business. Buckingham: SRHE.

Hou, Hou, Z. (2004) An investigation into the conceptions of information literacy among educational administrators in the University of Sheffield. Unpublished MSc dissertation. University of Sheffield. http://dagda.shef.ac.uk/dissertations/2003-04/External/Hou_Zhenqing_MScIM.pdf

Johnston, B. and Webber, S. (2004) "The role of LIS faculty in the information literate university: taking over the academy?" New library world, 105 (1/2), 12-20.

Johnston, B. and Webber, S. (2003) "Information literacy in higher education: a review and case study." Studies in higher education, 28 (3), 335-352.

Macfarlane, B. and Ottewill, R. (2001) Effective learning and teaching in business and management. London: Routledge.

Pedler, M., Boydell, T., Burgoyne, J. (1989), "Towards the learning company", Management Education and Development, Vol. 20 No.1, pp.1-8.

Town, S. (2003) "Information literacy: definition, measurement, impact." In: Martin, A. and Rader, H. (Eds) Information and IT literacy: enabling learning in the 21st Century. London: Fact. pp53-65.

Webber, S., Boon, S. and Johnston, B. (2005) "A comparison of UK academics' conceptions of information literacy in two disciplines: English and Marketing." Library and information research, 29 (93), 4-15.

Webber, S. and Johnston, B. (2005) "Information literacy in the curriculum: selected findings from a phenomenographic study of UK conceptions of, and pedagogy for, information literacy" In: Rust, C. (Ed) Improving Student Learning: Diversity and Inclusivity: Proceedings of the 11th ISL symposium, Birmingham, 6-8 September 2004. Oxford: Oxford Brookes University. pp212-224.

Appendix 1

1. Information Literacy: Embryonic

Students
- The majority of students would not recognise the concept of information literacy, and if they are information literate when they graduate, it is not something they are really aware of.
- If interviewed on the subject in their final year, they might see that information literacy is useful, but would agree with their lecturers that it would be difficult to fit it into the busy subject curriculum.

Management
- People mostly talk about information literacy "training" and about "giving people information skills".
- Information literacy is not mentioned as such in strategic documents, although some documents may contain statements which could imply interest in information literacy.
- Information literacy is not considered something which is of relevance in marketing the university.
- Senior managers confuse IT literacy and information literacy, and are most interested in the former.
- The management view of the library is focused on the resources it provides and on quantification of use (number of books borrowed, e-articles read etc).
- None of the key committees consider fostering information literacy as a key part of their remit.

Academics
- Most could not define "information literacy".
- Most are unwilling to give more than an hour of their class time to information literacy, and many will not even give that much.
- They assume that students will have certain information literacy knowledge/skills (e.g. the ability to find relevant articles, or to cite material properly) but most do not discuss these knowledge/skills with students. They may think that librarians are giving support or training in these areas, but if questioned they would admit that they do not have a good idea of what the librarians are actually doing.
- Most academics would be unwilling to involve librarians in curriculum design e.g. feeling that it was a waste of time or inappropriate.
- Librarians are chiefly perceived by them as service providers concerned with specific resources, such as books or e-journals.

Librarians
- Librarians are doing their own thing: there is a wide diversity of approach and attempts to coordinate are rather resented.
- The majority of librarians do not see education as a key role, and some of them positively dislike the idea of being educators. There is little discussion of

learning, teaching and assessment: it is the interest of a dedicated few. Most librarians do not have teaching qualifications.

- There is a variety of conceptions of information literacy. Many librarians focus on a few aspects of information literacy (e.g. searching), and may talk about "library skills".
- Librarians are concerned with efficiency, constraints, their low status, proving the cost-effectiveness of what they are doing.
- Most librarians either do not work with academics, or have limited contact (e.g. being asked to give a short introductory session to the library each year) and feel that they are not treated as peers.
- The person in charge of library and information services does not have a holistic conception of information literacy and/or does not see information literacy as a strategic issue that he/she needs to push forward.

Approach to Learning, Teaching and Assessment

- Information literacy training has not been embedded in most courses.
- In training sessions, the dominant approach is behaviourist (e.g. a presentation; a demonstration followed by a task following set steps).
- There is no clear distinction between assessment of student learning and evaluation of teaching: evaluation instruments cover both together.
- Assessment of information literacy is mostly not credit bearing, and in those few cases where it is, the percentage of marks awarded is very small (e.g. 5% of a class mark).
- Information literacy is taught mostly in short stand-alone sessions, or in very brief sessions within curricula.
- An online tutorial is seen as a good and sufficient solution to the "problem" of information literacy.
- Where assessment of students is considered, there is an emphasis on multiple choice questions, diagnostic tests, and compilation of bibliographies.
- There is little tailoring of information literacy training to specific level/discipline, except in terms of providing training on different subject databases.

2. Information Literacy: Intermediate

Management
- Information Literacy is part of a graduate attribute, but it is a minor part, or information literacy is not mentioned explicitly.
- The person responsible for information and library services is included in some strategic discussions, but not all.

Academics
- Some departments (e.g. law and medicine) are working with library staff on significant embedding of information literacy and identification of learning outcomes for information literacy at different levels.
- Some academics have a holistic conception of information literacy.
- Some academics see librarians as partners in educating their students.

Librarians

- There is a post (perhaps temporary) of "information Literacy Coordinator", who does not have line management responsibility for most (or any) of the staff who are engaged in information literacy work.
- Librarians are being asked to reflect and report on their information literacy work. Some do this enthusiastically and others reluctantly.
- There is reliance on informal channels to exchange experience and information between all those engaged in information literacy education.
- The relationship with academics is variable, with some resentment towards academics, who are still often seen as information illiterate.
- Some have teaching qualifications and/or have developed knowledge/skill in pedagogy, which also gives them confidence when collaborating with academics, but they are outnumbered by librarians who lack confidence in their teaching ability or who are unaware that they are poor teachers.

Approach to Learning, Teaching and Assessment

- Many people (academics, management, librarians) think that a generic approach to information literacy is sufficient and desirable.
- There is an online tutorial which most or all students have to go through, in some cases integrated into the curriculum. By some librarians and academics this is seen as a good and sufficient solution to the "problem" of information literacy.
- Information literacy education has been embedded in some courses, including linkage to credit-bearing assignments.
- The approach is moving away from the behaviourist, with increasing numbers of sessions in which a variety of teaching, learning and assessment methods are used. However short lectures and demonstration/set exercise sessions still dominate, standardisation is valued, and there is a tendency to see e.g. "the PowerPoints" as being the key teaching resources.
- Assessment of information literacy is mostly not credit bearing, and in those few cases where it is, the percentage of marks awarded is very small (e.g. 5% of a class mark).
- Information literacy is taught mostly in short stand-alone sessions, or in very brief sessions within curricula.

3. Towards the information literate university

Students

- Information Literacy is named as a Graduate Attribute.
- Students cannot graduate until they have demonstrated that they are information literate.
- Students understand what is meant by "information literacy" and can give an account of the stage they have reached in their education for information literacy.

- Students recognise the value of information literacy. They recognise it as a real subject of study upon which they have to expend effort in order to achieve success and they see its relevant to their future lives.

Management
- Information literacy is mentioned in strategic documents, such as the teaching and learning plan.
- The person with management responsibility for information and library services (i.e. including information literacy) is involved in decisions on, and is informed about, issues which are strategic to the university.
- A good information literacy programme is seen as a Unique Selling Proposition (USP) which the university mentions when it is promoting the university to prospective students etc. Librarians are involved in recruitment and retention campaigns.
- Academics and senior managers have an understanding of what information literacy is.
- People talk about information literacy "education" rather than "training".

Academics
- Discussion of/ information on Information literacy is included routinely as part of a new lecturer's induction programme.
- Academics cite their teaching of information literacy as evidence of their own good teaching (e.g. in applying for teaching excellence awards)
- Librarians work with academics in developing new courses and modules.
- Academics consult with them on information literacy education when changing a course.
- Academics respect librarians' expertise and use librarians as consultants in areas concerning information literacy.
- Academics and librarians have worked together to map information literacy progression into individual courses of study, and can indicate learning outcomes for each level of study.

Librarians
- Librarians, academics and students have a clear idea of their own and each others' involvement and responsibility in the learning process.
- A substantial proportion of librarians have "Information Literacy" in their job title and/or information literacy education is described in their job description as being a key part of their job.
- The majority of librarians understand and enjoy their role as educators, and are reflective practitioners, developing their own approach to teaching.
- Some librarians have teaching qualifications gained with the support of the library.
- There is regular discussion and exchange of experience amongst librarians about teaching, learning and assessment. There are formal and informal channels to foster sharing of experience.

- Librarians are able to identify good and bad teaching practice amongst their colleagues and academics, and are confident in their dealings with academics.
- There is collaboration with IT services and those providing academic support.
- All librarians have a good, holistic understanding of information literacy and many keep up-to-date with developments in the subject.

Approach to Learning, Teaching and Assessment
- Academics and librarians have worked together to map information literacy progression into individual courses of study, and can indicate learning outcomes for each level of study.
- Information literacy is assessed and assessed work is credit bearing.
- A variety of teaching learning and assessment modes and methods are used, as appropriate to the specific topic.

Reflections on the 'Information Literacy: recognising the need' conference at Staffordshire University, 17th May 2006

Mark Hepworth - Department of Information Science, Loughborough University

Although relatively few papers were presented at the Staffordshire conference analysing, synthesising and summarising contributions was challenging. Each paper was thought provoking and, together, they indicated and highlighted the complexity of the theoretical and pragmatic issues associated with information literacy. This complexity stems not only from the evolution of the concept itself; a notion that comes from, primarily, a positivistic and hence behaviourist conception of learning associated with coping in the library context but also, is inherently connected with a consciousness of the knowledge acquisition process and learning in general, and hence learning theory. Of the latter, the constructivist approach to learning by its nature leads to participative, experiential, problem based pedagogies that are currently the most practical approach to learning information literacy. An approach that is given even more weight due to the nature of an individual's change from information illiterate to information literate, equivalent to taking on board a new culture; a culture that fosters the independent lifelong learner. A change bound up with norms and values that go beyond the skills of finding and processing information; a change that is an individualised experience but, nevertheless, requires an appreciation and acceptance of socially identified, labelled, shared and, to some extent, agreed, knowledge, behaviours, attitudes, tools, techniques and processes. Furthermore this culture is far from static and is complicated by the rapidly changing technological environment that is associated with independent learning as well as the socio-economic context of globalisation, capitalism, democratisation; the data and information intensive nature of the knowledge based economy; the concomitant commodification of data, information and knowledge; and the associated ideas of consumerism, personalisation and inclusion. Hence information literacy is, as Andretta and also Webber & Johnston indicate, a *'profound education issue'* that is connected to a host of factors, as indicated above.

Cultural, individual and technological barriers to information literacy and independent learning are therefore the concern of our profession which is intrinsically concerned with facilitating peoples' interaction and management of this reality. This is reflected in the individual contributions to this conference. At an epistemological level the prevalent positivist and related behaviourist, didactic conception of learning found in most educational institutions is seen as an obstacle. This was exemplified by Webber & Johnston's discussion of the challenge to information literacy in an Australian university due to the new Head of Learning and Teaching's concern about the quantification and measurability of information literacy and the desire of educators and administrators for accountability highlighted by Brauer. In addition there is a paternalistic view, that it is necessary to 'spoon feed' the widening group of students many of whom do not come from backgrounds where parents were lucky enough to have developed an independent learning mentality, due to their education, upbringing or personal experience, and have communicated this to their children.

Brauer gave further evidence for this positivistic view of learning citing the evidence-based approach to medical information that promotes the conception of 'truth' that may limit the creative process of knowledge creation. Andretta extends this to the wider 'political' level and the perceived threat of independent learning and the information literacy component to current power structures. That information literacy and independent learning is seen as a threat to the status, authority and power of academics and librarians due to its empowerment of the student and making them less dependent on the people currently employed by the academic institutions. She argues that the scrapping of the Higher Education Orientation Module at London Metropolitan University is a consequence of this.

Another barrier, not explicitly stated but indicated in the quotations from academics in Webber & Johnston's paper, is the academics' and University administrators' lack of consciousness or systematic knowledge of current and established theories of learning as well as their limited understanding of the concept information literacy. Understanding theories such as those of Kolb, Bloom etc. would tend to, inevitably, lead to a desire to encourage independent, self-motivated, reflective, experiential problem-based learning and the development of learning environments where students can construct their own and shared independent learning culture through interaction with and manipulation of data, information and knowledge.

Goodwin and also Brauer discuss the current and evolving technological environment where search engines are a barrier to developing information literacy and independent learning. The simplistic, two-word, mode of searching that Google (and other search engines) have encouraged and the relatively uncritical assembly of data and information, despite or perhaps because of the ranking algorithms, and has 'dumbed down' the searcher. The fact that the learner can 'get by' entering a few terms does not encourage thinking about and trying to conceptualise and define a search topic. Furthermore that these tools have in fact narrowed the range of learning resources, discouraging the use of books, paper sources and the serendipitous nature of the first hand, 'real world', exploitation of other environments such as museums, galleries etc. This raises the interesting conundrum that the portal effect i.e. the bringing together of 'authorised' resources in the virtual learning environments (VLEs) may also exacerbate this situation. All the students 'needs' are satisfied 'on a plate' which may echo a lack of confidence and faith in our young learners, as Andretta points out. The VLE may only serve to develop the independence of the learner to some extent or at worst to limit their independent learning experience. However, from a pragmatic perspective, society or society's social engineers, may deem that the chance to raise the information literacy level of the wider population is good enough for the knowledge-based economy and that more sophisticated forms of information literacy may only be needed by a minority who gain their education in the few elitist institutions.

The need to address the evident lack of conscious knowledge of academics and administrators in higher education (and perhaps the same could be said of many involved with the delivery of primary and secondary education) and the need to address this are found in other papers given at the conference. Bent, Higgins and Brettel focus on engaging staff in a discourse about information literacy. This discourse will help to foster the development of an environment in which students can explore their information literacy. Webber & Johnston's study that involved discussing with academics their perceptions of information literacy is in, a way, further evidence that this discourse is necessary and is underway elsewhere.

The creation of an environment that helps the individual to develop their information literacy and enables academics to provide appropriate learning environments is also found in Bent, Higgins and Brettel's paper as well Jones, Peter and Shields and in Goodwin's. Again Goodwin highlights the challenge associated with Google but also notes that Google and Google Scholar is part of the current learning reality. We cannot ignore Google and Google Scholar so educators need to adapt to this environment, utilize and not dismiss it. He argues that generic skills and knowledge traditionally associated with information literacy need to be emphasised because of this new context, for example, the need to rigorously investigate the quality and authority of information and to put greater emphasis on defining information need since this may be undervalued or overlooked due to the ease of searching with Google and Google Scholar. The role of other evolving tools, Goodwin argues, may also need to be recognised, for example, the use of blogs to foster discourse about information literacy and discourse in general between students. Yahoo groups may serve a similar purpose. With regard to helping the academics/teachers Bent, Higgins and Brettel also discuss the development of tools that would help them create effective learning environments where students could experience information literacy and associated dispositions. This included the development of a suite of learning tools based on SCONUL's seven pillars conception of information literacy.

Similarly Jones, Peter and Shields address the issue of motivation and the need to engage and impress students as well as impress faculty staff through the use of interactive whiteboards. They found that interactive whiteboards helped to engage and motivate students because it was new technology; it encouraged active learning through live annotation. Active learning, as well as reflection, were also encouraged through the use of games and voting (a form of quiz) which were facilitated by the interactive whiteboards. They also argued that the use of this technology helped improve their status in the eyes of the learner and academics, which in turn helped with the effective delivery of information literacy. The creation of learning environments for teaching staff, in addition to the pedagogic environment, is important since although well-intentioned academics may not have the knowledge of what is possible. They may even suffer from technophobia and, of course, a lack of time. The latter is due to the commercialisation of the academic environment, the increased numbers of students, and the ongoing desire of administrators to get 'more out of the same pint pot' i.e. the academics and support staff.

In conclusion it can be seen that a host of issues have a bearing on information literacy from the global, political and economic to the engagement of the individual in the learning process. Reflecting on this landscape and the apparent need to change the current physical and pedagogic landscape if information literacies and independent learning are to be fostered, a number of questions come to mind:

- Do our educational institutions genuinely want to encourage the independent, lifelong learner? How do we deal with the apparent perceived threat to teaching and academia posed by the independent learner? How do we foster more dialogue about these issues in the educational sector? How can the fears about accountability and assessment be addressed that is associated with a shift from an emphasis on a positivistic, behaviourist pedagogy to one that places more faith in a constructivist approach? Should we lobby for those in education to be better educated in learning theory as well as independent learning and information literacy?
- What level of information literacy does our society want and among whom? Everyone? The few? Webber & Johnston's description of levels of an information literate university has a bearing on this.
- What form should the physical environment take? How do we avoid creating environments that have the effect of 'dumbing down' or 'spoon feeding' the learner?
- Should we, as a profession, broaden our focus to include the wider topic of independent learning rather than focus on the subset of information literacy? If so do we need to develop the knowledge and skills associated with the management of not just information but data and knowledge? Do we also need to extend our knowledge of learning, learning theory and pedagogy? Without this it may be difficult to communicate with educators, limiting our impact and make it hard to facilitate change and help create environments that empower the individual as an independent learner.

These are the issues that need to be discussed by information professionals, educators and educational administrators. Without the discussion and resolution of these issues, by the various stakeholders, it is likely that an unsatisfactory, piecemeal approach to helping learners to be independent learners will continue to be the case.

Acknowledgment:

I would like to thank the conference organisers and contributors for giving me the opportunity and the 'fodder' to think about these issues and other academics and practitioners who have helped stimulate these thoughts. It should be noted that this article represents my interpretation of others' contributions to the conference as well as my own opinions. I would therefore hasten to apologise to any contributors, to the Staffordshire University conference on '*Information Literacy: recognising the need*', who may feel that I have misrepresented their views.